John Omer

101 GAMES
FOR TRAINERS

A Collection of the Best Activities from
Creative Training Techniques Newsletter

by Bob Pike with Christopher Busse

Copyright © 1995, 2004 by Bob Pike and Lakewood Publications

Published by: HRD Press, Inc.
                 22 Amherst Road
                 Amherst, MA 01002
                 1-800-822-2801 (U.S. and Canada)
                 413-253-3488
                 413-253-3490 (fax)
                 www.hrdpress.com

ISBN 0-943210-38-0

Contents

Foreword

This book, *101 Games for Trainers,* is one in a series drawn from the best content of *Creative Training Techniques Newsletter.* The newsletter was conceived in 1988 by editor and internationally known trainer Bob Pike to be a one-stop resource of practical "how-tos" for trainers. The idea was (and still is) to provide timely tips, techniques, and strategies that help trainers with the special tasks they perform daily.

When the newsletter began, it was largely fueled by Bob's 20 years of experience in the field and by the best ideas shared by the trainers (more than 50,000 in all) who had attended his Creative Training Techniques seminars. As the newsletter grew in popularity, it also began to draw on ideas submitted by its readers. Today, the newsletter continues to search out creative approaches from the more than 200 seminars Bob and the other Creative Training Techniques trainers conduct every year, and from the more than 10,000 newsletter readers.

But no matter where the insights originate, the goal of the newsletter remains the same: To provide trainers a cafeteria of ideas they can quickly absorb, choosing those that best suit their special needs.

As stated earlier, this series of books represents the best ideas from *Creative Training Techniques Newsletter*'s seven years of publication. It is our hope that we've created a valuable resource you'll come back to again and again to help address the unique challenges you face daily in your role as a trainer.

Sincerely,

The Editors

Introduction

The time I've spent in adult classrooms over the years led me to create something I call "Pike's Five Laws of Adult Learning." Perhaps the most important law in that list is the Third Law:

Learning is directly proportional to the amount of fun you have.

Let's face it. If your participants are going to learn anything in your classroom—and then retain that information once they leave—injecting fun into your session is imperative. In this age of entertainment, you will rarely run into a person who would prefer that you simply stand at a podium and *teach*. I believe the true joy of learning comes from involvement and participation.

That's why I think you'll find *101 Games for Trainers* invaluable. The exercises and activities here are specifically designed to actively involve trainees by breaking the ice and grabbing participants' attention, bringing a weary group back to life, developing communication skills, promoting teamwork, leading an audience through a spirited review session, or addressing the special concerns of certain topical courses.

And because these exercises represent the best of the ideas collected in *Creative Training Techniques Newsletter*, you know they have been successfully used in corporate classrooms all over the world. With each exercise, a brief description of its purpose is provided, as well as a reference for the amount of time the exercise will take, the ideal group size for the exercise, and a checklist of materials you will need to make the exercise happen.

Defining the Categories

The exercises in this book fall into one or more of these six categories. Just below the title of each exercise, you'll find a listing of these six categories. The small checkmarks beside each of the categories serve as guides for where best to use the exercise.

Please remember, however, that these are only suggestions. With the right amount of imagination, the exercises here can be adapted to suit almost any training need.

Openers

These exercises, commonly known as "ice breakers," serve as vehicles for getting participants to introduce themselves or for putting trainees into the right "frame of mind" for the coming session.

These exercises might vary according to the type of training being conducted, how big the group is, and how well the group members know each other.

Also keep in mind the Law of Primacy: People remember best what we do first, so choose your openers carefully. (To be honest, nearly all of the exercises here could be adapted as some form of opener.)

Energizers

Designed to involve a group *actively,* these mid-course exercises are best used during the infamous mid-afternoon slump or anytime you feel a group's attention might be waning.

Often, these games take the form of energetic review sessions or stimulating brainteasers, or even a physical activity that gets people up and moving. The secret here is that these exercises aren't always planned.

The best strategy in developing a course is to have a handful of relevant energizers ready to go at a moment's notice and implement one when you see attention begin to slip.

Communication

Use these exercises to make a point to trainees about the importance of communication, or to show where certain communication skills need improvement. Exercises that help enhance listening skills also fall into this category. As with "Openers," a great many of the activities in this book could easily be adapted to make a point about communication skills, depending on how you position them.

Team-building

The purpose of these exercises is to help improve the relationship of individuals within a group— either a specific "work group" or simply a small group formed during your training session. These exercises are extremely challenging for trainers because

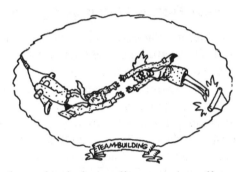

they call for participants to work independently in small groups (usually solving some sort of problem) for periods of time that exceed other types of exercises. Your challenge is to keep things moving and to monitor closely the progress of the groups.

Review

The last words any group of trainees wants to hear are, "Okay, let's review." To keep participants from completely tuning out, these exercises often help disguise a review session as a light, interactive competition. *One word of caution:* When the competitive juices of some attendees get flowing, things can easily get out of hand. Your challenge is to keep the competition light and—whenever possible—to promote *cooperation* rather than competition.

Topical

One of the challenges trainers face is finding games and exercises that pertain to a certain kind of session (customer service or diversity training, for example). While many other exercises can be adapted for those kinds of training, we've identified several

"topical" games that work particularly well in specific situations.

A Few Words About Using These Games

Whether it's the first time or the five hundredth time you've used games in your classroom, I believe there are some fundamentals you should be aware of when implementing these exercises.

▼ **Assess your audience and know the risks.** Some of the following exercises will be natural hits with certain types of audiences, but others might bomb. Ultimately, it's up to you to decide what kind of game to play with what kind of audience. But you also need to assess your own comfort level with "pulling off" these games. A rule of thumb: If you're even remotely uncomfortable with an exercise, don't use it. Participants will sense your hesitation and share your discomfort.

▼ **Never use a game without debriefing afterward.** It might be obvious to *you* how a game enhances your subject matter, but it's dangerous to assume your participants are on the same page. Follow every game with a debriefing session to help participants ease back into the session itself, see the transition you've attempted to create, and assimilate the game's learning points.

▼ **Be creative. Adapt, adapt, adapt.** Nothing about *any* game in this book is set in stone. The trainers to whom these ideas are attributed were successful in using these games because they adapted the exercises to suit their own needs.

Though you'll be able to pluck many of them right off the page and insert them into your sessions, I challenge you to make these games uniquely your own whenever you can. The result will be an exercise that has even more relevance to you, your company, and your classroom. But most important, the result will be an exercise that's more *fun*.

101 Games for Trainers

❖ ❖ ❖

A Collection
of the Best Activities
from
Creating Training Techniques
Newsletter

❖ ❖

GAME #1: The Other Half

Game Categories:
☑ Opener   ☐ Team-building
☐ Energizer   ☐ Review
☐ Communication   ☐ Topical

❖ **Purpose:** To pair participants for a series of personal introductions at the outset of class.

❖ **Time Required:** 5 minutes.

❖ **Size of Group:** Unlimited (but since it calls for an even number of participants, you may have to take part in your own game).

❖ **Materials Required:** A number of small index cards, prepared in advance by the trainer.

❖ **The Exercise in Action:** Jeri Eberhardt, senior instructor for Computer Task Group, Buffalo, NY, shuffles a deck of prepared index cards and asks participants to select one. Written on each card is a word that is one-half of a well-known or logical pair.

The participants' task is to move around the room and find their "other half." Here are some examples of words Eberhardt uses on the paired cards:

- Rise / Shine
- Bacon / Eggs
- Mr. / Mrs.
- War / Peace
- Trial / Error
- Pork chops / Applesauce

Once pairs are matched, participants interview their partners and introduce each other to the class.

GAME #2: Mystery Shopping

Game Categories:
- ☐ Opener
- ☐ Energizer
- ☑ Communication
- ☐ Team-building
- ☐ Review
- ☑ Topical: Customer Service

❖ **Purpose:** To sensitize front-line employees to the importance of solid customer service, problem-solving, and telephone skills.

❖ **Time Required:** 15 minutes per day during a multi-day workshop on customer service skills.

❖ **Size of Group:** Unlimited.

❖ **Materials Required:** None.

❖ **The Exercise in Action:** "Mystery shopping" and "mystery calling" activities help focus customer service training, according to Helen Socha, vice president at Worth Bank & Trust, Worth, IL. The following two activities teach front-line employees—especially new-hires—the difference between good and poor customer service skills, problem-solving skills, and telephone techniques by putting them in the customers' shoes.

▼ For the mystery shopping exercise, Socha sends pairs of participants to "shop" at a local mall with a checklist of good and bad customer service behaviors to watch for. As mystery shoppers, they observe and record the clerks' customer service skills at a fast-food restaurant, specialty store, or department store. The teams present their experiences back in class. Socha then leads a discussion about their experiences by asking: What were the differences in service between stores? Among service representatives? Was service adequate, above average, or excellent? Why?

Participants are sent to "mystery shop" at retail stores instead of competitor banks, Socha says, to keep participants from clouding the service issue by comparing products and equipment instead of representatives' behaviors.

▼ For the mystery calling activity, Socha gives each participant a list of businesses and shops to call about their products or services. She then conducts a discussion of the differences among the representatives at each of the businesses, using the same line of questioning and discussion as with the mystery shopping activity.

GAME #3: The Sum of All Fears

Game Categories:
- ☐ Opener
- ☑ Energizer
- ☐ Communication
- ☐ Team-building
- ☐ Review
- ☐ Topical

◆ **Purpose:** To show participants the consequences of jumping to conclusions and making assumptions without careful consideration.

◆ **Time Required:** 10 minutes.

◆ **Size of Group:** Unlimited.

◆ **Materials Required:** A prepared transparency (see graphic below).

◆ **The Exercise in Action:** John Erwin, a consultant for Master Planning Group International in Edina, MN, posts the following addition problem on a transparency, but reveals only the top figure:

```
      1,000
         40
      1,000
         30
      1,000
         20
      1,000
+        10
```

He tells the group that the object of the game is for the class as a whole to add each number from top to bottom, saying the total aloud as he reveals the subsequent numbers. As he uncovers the last figure, Erwin asks the class for a total. Most of the participants blurt out, "5,000." He repeats the process a few more times and then uncovers all figures so they can see them all at once. They then discover that the sum is 4,100.

Erwin discusses with the class how easy it is to come to a conclusion that seems crystal clear, yet still be completely wrong. He reminds participants to stay open-minded and to look at all options before passing judgment.

GAME #4: Jellybean Jamboree

Game Categories:
☐ Opener ☐ Team-building
☐ Energizer ☐ Review
☐ Communication ☑ Topical: Diversity

❖ **Purpose:** To demonstrate the extent of diversity in work groups, especially in small ones.

❖ **Time Required:** 10 minutes.

❖ **Size of Group:** Unlimited.

❖ **Materials Required:** Paper cups; assorted flavors of jelly beans; index cards.

❖ **The Exercise in Action:** George Wilson, president of Lovoy's Team Works, Birmingham, AL, places a number of paper cups on a large table. Each cup contains a different flavor of jellybean. In front of each cup is an index card labeled with a distinct demographic or human characteristic reflecting differences in ethnicity, gender, age, place of birth, or personality type. For example: Born in the Northeast, under 25 years old, outgoing/expressive, has African roots, detail-oriented thinker.

At an appropriate point in the session, ideally just before an afternoon break, participants are given paper cups and instructed to visit the display and take one jellybean from each cup that reflects a characteristic that is present in their work group.

After counting their jellybeans and recording the number, participants may enjoy them as a snack. After the break, Wilson leads a discussion on workforce diversity and how to help diversity thrive, using the jellybean exercise to demonstrate the diversity that exists even in very small groups.

If the cost of jellybeans is a problem, other candies, such as M&Ms or Skittles, can be substituted.

GAME #5: Sequencing

Game Categories:
- ☐ Opener
- ☑ Energizer
- ☐ Communication
- ☐ Team-building
- ☐ Review
- ☐ Topical

❖ **Purpose:** To initiate a discussion on creativity, problem-solving, decision-making, or perceptions.

❖ **Time Required:** 20 minutes.

❖ **Size of Group:** Unlimited.

❖ **Materials Required:** Five index cards per participant, prepared in advance by the trainer.

❖ **The Exercise in Action:** Leo Smigelski, manager of instructor training and training evaluations with Westinghouse Hanford Co., Richland, WA, gives each participant a set of five index cards, each listing one year, one letter, and one number chosen randomly from the following subsets: one year from the chronological sequence 1775, 1776, 1777, 1778, and 1779; one letter from the sequence, A, B, C, D, and E; and one number from the sequence 3, 7, 12, 17, and 25.

He then tells participants to "put the cards in order," giving no other instructions, allowing them two minutes to complete the exercise. Participants then report how they ordered their cards. Most order the cards alphabetically using the A–E sequence, a few use the "historical" sequence, and nearly all see the third numerical sequence as "random." Smigelski then leads a discussion on why participants order the cards as they do (they base their sequence on assumptions about order), why they did not order them in one of the other ways possible (possibly locked into familiar procedures), and what rules should be followed when sequencing (discuss alternatives).

Finally, he moves the discussion to the importance of approaching creative activities without making assumptions about their structure. He discusses looking for alternatives, the importance of going from familiar to unfamiliar, and not being locked in by official documents/procedures.

Smigelski says the activity helps participants realize that in processing information in a lesson, they often make assumptions about the way it should be sequenced, using preconceived ideas and blocking out creativity.

GAME #6: Musical Chairs with a Twist

Game Categories:	☐ Opener	☐ Team-building
	☐ Energizer	☐ Review
	☑ Communication	☑ Topical

❖ **Purpose:** To use a familiar children's game as a model for lessons in change and conflict.

❖ **Time Required:** 20 minutes.

❖ **Size of Group:** 10 to 15.

❖ **Materials Required:** Chairs for each participant; a portable CD or audiotape player.

❖ **The Exercise in Action:** Believe it or not, the childhood game of musical chairs enables people to feel the effects of change, but in a nonthreatening environment, says Mary Walter, an education coordinator at HBO & Co., Atlanta.

The game is based on the "scarcity premise." There is always one less chair than there are participants in need of chairs. In the well-known game, music is played while the participants move clockwise around a circle of chairs. When the music stops, everyone scrambles for a chair. The person left standing must leave the game and become an observer. One chair is removed each time the music is stopped. This continues until only one participant remains.

The familiar exercise can take two directions, Walter says. In sessions on change management, her objective is to bring out and address emotional issues that emerge during change. Several rounds into the game, she asks participants to pay particular attention to the feelings they experience during the remaining rounds.

After the exercise, she asks participants to share their thoughts on the emotions they feel and on the behavior they witness in others. The conversation, Walter says, makes people aware of feelings they might not otherwise acknowledge, and shows them that others feel the same stresses.

If the focus of the session is communication and its importance in an environment of change, she begins by making it very obvious when she is going to stop the music. She turns very deliberately toward the tape or record player and reaches for the appropriate control.

Later in the game (or in a second round), she takes the opposite tack, keeping her hand on the controls at all times, making no eye contact, even using music with deceptive pauses to deceive participants.

The conversation following this version of the exercise centers on the different reactions people experience as a result of the two communication styles. Participants can usually offer examples of parallel situations in everyday corporate life.

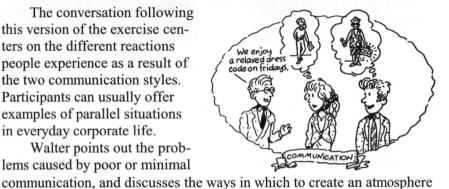

Walter points out the problems caused by poor or minimal communication, and discusses the ways in which to create an atmosphere of open communication.

GAME #7: The Secret Word

Game Categories:
- ☐ Opener
- ☐ Energizer
- ☑ Communication
- ☐ Team-building
- ☑ Review
- ☐ Topical

❖ **Purpose:** To provide an incentive for participants to listen more closely to course content.

❖ **Time Required:** About 15 minutes of trainer preparation time.

❖ **Size of Group:** Unlimited.

❖ **Materials Required:** Cardboard-type material to create placard; string; bright markers or paint.

❖ **The Exercise in Action:** Before class begins, Jacqueline O'Neill, a training supervisor with Whitehall-Robins in Hammonton, NJ, hangs a dangling, two-sided placard from the ceiling near the blackboard area (to discourage peekers). On the side facing participants she paints brightly colored question marks of various sizes to grab the group's attention. On the side facing away she writes one key word or phrase from the course.

O'Neill encourages the group to listen intently throughout the session for particular key words or phrases relating to important themes, then jot them on their paper. But she doesn't let on as to why they're doing it, only that it's important.

At the close of the session, O'Neill reveals the placard's purpose: on it is written the "secret word" relating to class content. Referring to their jotted notes, participants are asked to call out at random what they think the word is. The first to guess the word is rewarded with a voucher for a free lunch or another token gift.

Game Categories:
- ☐ Opener
- ☐ Energizer
- ☐ Communication
- ☐ Team-building
- ☐ Review
- ☑ Topical: Diversity

❖ **Purpose:** To broaden participants' definition of "diversity."

❖ **Time Required:** 10 minutes.

❖ **Size of Group:** Unlimited.

❖ **Materials Required:** A box of "multicultural" Crayola crayons. (The special set, containing all the colors that can be used as skin tones, is available through Chaselle, Inc., 800-242-7355.)

❖ **The Exercise in Action:** People often tend to think of diversity in terms of race or gender, overlooking the less obvious differences, such as age, geographic background, and so on, says Sharon Lovoy. She starts diversity training sessions with an exercise designed to help people recognize that every individual is unique and that diversity issues often go beyond the obvious.

She pairs off participants and asks them to work with their partners to list the differences between them—hair color, education level, date of birth, and whatever else they notice.

After two or three minutes, Lovoy stops the exercise and locates the team with the longest list. She has one of them read their list to the class. Their prize is a box each of "multicultural" Crayola crayons.

Game Categories:
- [ ] Opener
- [ ] Energizer
- [x] Communication
- [x] Team-building
- [ ] Review
- [ ] Topical

❖ **Purpose:** To teach participants the importance of clear communication and the dangers of relying on preconceptions.

❖ **Time Required:** 10 to 15 minutes.

❖ **Size of Group:** Best in a group of 20, with participants working in four teams of five.

❖ **Materials Required:** Masking tape; four long pieces of light, sturdy rope or clothesline (at least 10 feet in length); a sturdy metal ring; a red scarf or other bright marker.

❖ **The Exercise in Action:** May Akamine, director of outpatient services and chief nursing officer at Castle Medical Center in Kailua, HI, uses a "tug-of-war" activity to build teamwork and improve communication skills:

In the middle of the space for the activity, use tape to mark a 1-foot square. Tie the scarf and one end of each rope to the ring. Place the ring in the middle of the taped-off square with the ropes extended out in four directions (see diagram).

Divide the class into four teams and have each team hold onto a rope. Give the teams these guidelines: "The purpose of this activity is to get as many points as possible in 30 seconds. A point is scored each time the marker crosses a line. You have 30 seconds to talk about it."

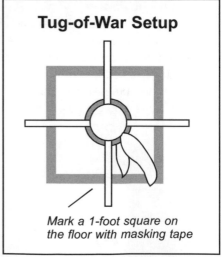

Tug-of-War Setup

Mark a 1-foot square on the floor with masking tape

When the "competition" begins, Akamine says the teams usually start tugging at the rope to get points for their own teams. After 30 seconds, she asks them how many points they have. The teams usually have few or no points. Akamine repeats the activity, giving the guidelines again, explicitly. Usually, she says, the teams start to ask questions about the guidelines and the purpose of the activity. The teams eventually realize the activity is a cooperative effort, not a competition, and that they must work together to pile up points by moving the scarf rapidly in a circle over the taped box.

GAME #10: Standing Around

Game Categories:

☐	Opener	☐	Team-building
☐	Energizer	☐	Review
☐	Communication	☑	Topical: Customer Service

❖ **Purpose:** To raise sensitivity about customers' resistance to standing in line.

❖ **Time Required:** 5 minutes.

❖ **Size of Group:** Unlimited.

❖ **Materials Required:** None.

❖ **The Exercise in Action:** Teri Robertson training coordinator for Sea World of Florida, Orlando, FL, says the park uses this exercise in customer service training to raise sensitivity in employees about a pet peeve of many customers: being kept waiting while workers attend to seemingly more "important" tasks. Continuing to talk on the phone while customers wait for service is a good example.

Workshop participants are first told that each of them is responsible for ensuring that guests visiting the park have a good time. At that point, Robertson instructs everyone to stand up, stand on only one foot, and not to put down the other foot until told to do so.

Robertson then proceeds to leisurely page through class notes with her back to participants. She then announces she has to make an important phone call, and walks out of the room. After returning a few minutes later, participants are told, finally, that they can put down their foot.

Robertson then makes the point: while participants have been left standing *physically,* customers are often left standing *figuratively.* "Any time we give guests the idea that other things besides their needs take precedence, we leave them standing on one foot," Robertson says.

Like some participants, some customers will continue to patiently "stand on one foot" until the employee returns, but they will probably later tell everyone within earshot how uncomfortable they've been made to feel. Other people will immediately put down that foot and vent their displeasure with the first employee to happen by, whether he or she is responsible for the problem or not.

"If all employees realize the importance of giving guests the attention they deserve, we can avoid the 'foot problems' we all encounter at public facilities," Robertson says.

GAME #11: Personal Lifelines

Game Categories:	☑ Opener	☐ Team-building
	☐ Energizer	☐ Review
	☐ Communication	☐ Topical

❖ **Purpose:** To help participants get to know one another beyond name and job title.

❖ **Time Required:** 20 to 30 minutes.

❖ **Size of Group:** 6 to 10.

❖ **Materials Required:** Paper and writing utensils for all participants.

❖ **The Exercise in Action:** Michael Mezack, director of continuing education and associate professor of educational psychology and leadership at Texas Tech University, Lubbock, TX, asks participants to draw a line on a piece of paper (or several pieces attached end-to-end, if necessary) representing their lives to date. At the far left end, participants fill in their year of birth. The other end is marked with the present date.

Participants then record important life events along that line—personal, professional, or simply interesting—with an eye toward illustrating what brought them to where they are today.

Next they take turns explaining their lifelines to the group. It might be wise to set a time limit per person if time is a factor, Mezack says. Afterward, participants may post their charts on classroom walls for others to review at their leisure.

To get people started, Mezack displays and explains his own lifeline, making it clear that people may be as candid or reserved as is comfortable. This technique, he says, is especially useful in smaller groups, since explaining the lifelines can take several minutes per participant.

GAME #12: Competitive Review

Game Categories:

- ☐ Opener
- ☐ Energizer
- ☐ Communication
- ☐ Team-building
- ☑ Review
- ☐ Topical

❖ **Purpose:** To inject an element of competition into review sessions during multi-day courses.

❖ **Time Required:** As long as one hour, depending on the amount of material being reviewed.

❖ **Size of Group:** Unlimited, but participants should work in small groups of three to eight.

❖ **Materials Required:** Test questions prepared in advance by the trainer.

❖ **The Exercise in Action:** Rather than the standard practice of giving a test at the end of each day of his five-day training sessions, grading it, and then reviewing results the next day in class, David Blunt, international training and sales development manager for Alcon Surgical Laboratories in Fort Worth, TX, uses this technique:

Blunt cuts out individual questions from a prepared test and places them in an envelope. The envelope is then passed from small group to small group, with each group removing one question and posing it to another group. Each group receives the same number of chances to answer questions. If the question is not answered correctly by the targeted group, all other groups get a chance to answer. At the end of the exercise, the group with the most correct answers receives a small prize.

GAME #13: The Boob Tube

Game Categories:
- ☐ Opener
- ☑ Energizer
- ☐ Communication
- ☐ Team-building
- ☐ Review
- ☐ Topical

❖ **Purpose:** To energize participants mid-course and form new small groups.

❖ **Time Required:** 5 minutes.

❖ **Size of Group:** Unlimited.

❖ **Materials Required:** Slips of paper and flipcharts prepared in advance by the trainer.

❖ **The Exercise in Action:** Instead of having participants simply number off to form small groups, James Kast, a computer specialist at USDA, Office of Finance Management, National Finance Center, in New Orleans, lets each participant select a piece of paper that has a name of a character from a TV show. He then has them find the shows to which they belong by matching their slips with the appropriate show names posted in different areas of the classroom. For example, for the show *Gilligan's Island,* the characters Ginger, the Skipper, Mary Ann, the Professor, etc., would all work together.

As a variation to forming new groups, have participants find other people with characters from the same show without the help of a poster with the show's title hanging on the wall.

GAME #14: Benchmarking the Best

Game Categories:
☐ Opener
☐ Energizer
☐ Communication
☐ Team-building
☐ Review
☑ Topical: Supervisory

❖ **Purpose:** To demonstrate to supervisors the value of benchmarking as a quality improvement tool.

❖ **Time Required:** 20 minutes on each day of a multi-session course.

❖ **Size of Group:** Unlimited, but participants should work in small groups of four to eight.

❖ **Materials Required:** Flipchart paper; markers for small groups.

❖ **The Exercise in Action:** Participants in Richard Wittkopf's multi-session management skills course benchmark themselves against what they perceive to be the ideal manager.

Wittkopf, director of corporate training and development at Liquid Air, Walnut Creek, CA, breaks participants into small groups, asking them to brainstorm the key management skills of the best manager/supervisor they have worked for and list those attributes on flipchart sheets. The entire class then votes for the 15 most important attributes. Next, Wittkopf asks participants to rate themselves on each of the 15 skills on a scale of 1 to 10, with 1 = low rating and 10 = high rating. After rating themselves, participants identify their three greatest challenges and three greatest strengths.

Between training sessions, Wittkopf has participants ask their managers, a peer, and three or four direct reports to rate the participant's management skills. Participants bring those ratings to class and discuss them with their peers. At the end of the multi-session management course, participants evaluate themselves again on each of the 15 skills to see how they've improved. Wittkopf also encourages participants to ask the same work associates to rate them again to see how they've changed.

This idea can be adapted to other types of training, including customer service skills, presentation skills, and communication skills, by substituting the attributes discussed.

Game Categories:
- ☐ Opener
- ☑ Energizer
- ☐ Communication
- ☑ Team-building
- ☐ Review
- ☐ Topical

❖ **Purpose:** To break taboos about solving problems as a team.

❖ **Time Required:** 10 to 20 minutes.

❖ **Size of Group:** Unlimited.

❖ **Materials Required:** Prepared brainteasers.

What do you see in this picture?

❖ **The Exercise in Action:** When employees cling to taboos about solving problems as part of a team rather than on their own, companies lose opportunities for significant gains, says James Healy, executive vice president for KSF Associates, Inc., in Cedar Rapids, IA.

He uses illusions—such as the classic "old woman/young woman" exercise at right—as a tool to encourage participants to think beyond the obvious in solving problems in their business environments. (**Note:** the old woman's nose is the young woman's cheek.) After completing a few of these on their own, participants are asked two questions: Did anyone get all of them figured out? Did some of you get at least one figured out? Healy says participants typically answer no to the first question, and yes to the second.

He then asks the group how they each could have solved all of the illusions. They usually say by helping one another, sharing ideas, and working as a team. When Healy asks why they didn't do that, they cite the belief—ingrained from a young age—"that they must keep their eyes on their own papers, do their own work, and that information sharing is cheating." He makes the point that people working in groups often accomplish what one person working alone cannot.

Healy says it's important that trainers do not, at any point in the exercise, admonish participants to do their own work. "Believe me, they will assume that on their own," he says.

GAME #16: Secret Roles

Game Categories:	☐ Opener	☑ Team-building
	☐ Energizer	☐ Review
	☑ Communication	☐ Topical

❖ **Purpose:** To show participants how different roles and communication styles affect group dynamics.

❖ **Time Required:** 15 to 20 minutes.

❖ **Size of Group:** Unlimited, but participants should work in small groups of four.

❖ **Materials Required:** Envelopes and "job descriptions" prepared in advance by the trainer.

❖ **The Exercise in Action:** Paul Bernard, a corporate management skills trainer at K-Mart Corp., in East Brunswick, NJ, rotates participants through a series of "roles" in group-based activities to help people see firsthand the value of the different roles and communication styles assumed in group situations.

Upon arriving at his workshops, each participant is given an envelope with "Do Not Open" written on the outside and is assigned a seat, typically within a group of four. After the workshop begins and introductions are completed, participants are asked to open their envelopes and read the contents silently.

Typed on a slip of paper inside the envelopes are "jobs" that partici-pants are asked to perform during small-group exercises, and accompany-ing job descriptions. Some job titles include: *Mr. Can Do Positive Attitude* (responsible for countering any negative statements made during the meeting with a positive statement), *Group Leader* (asked to keep group on the subject and maximize participation), *Question Asker* (given pre-selected questions to ask throughout the exercise), and *Time Keeper* (responsible for ensuring that the group members stay on schedule). Each group has a similar set of job titles at its table.

The "catch" to the exercise, Bernard says, is that no one at the table is allowed to divulge their job title, just perform it. Participants may ask others what motivates them to do their jobs, but job titles cannot be revealed until the end of the exercise (although many are correctly guessed). When new small groups are formed, the game starts anew as participants take on different roles.

Bernard says the exercise "creates added participation and improves concentration."

GAME #17: Balloon Break

Game Categories:	☐ Opener	☐ Team-building
	☑ Energizer	☐ Review
	☑ Communication	☐ Topical

❖ **Purpose:** To inject humor into long, multi-session training courses and keep participants alert.

❖ **Time Required:** 2 to 5 minutes per participant.

❖ **Size of Group:** Unlimited.

❖ **Materials Required:** Helium-filled balloons with inserted question slips prepared in advance by the trainer.

❖ **The Exercise in Action:** At various points during a comprehensive, two-week program, Ken Kuplic uses an energizer that breaks the monotony, but also makes a learning point—something of a rarity with energizers.

Kuplic, a claims training instructor for Sentry Insurance Co., Stevens Point, WI, prepares two or three helium-filled balloons per participant before the session begins, planting a slip of paper with a topic written on it in each balloon before inflating it. The topics range from the absurd ("Explain why geese fly in a vee formation," for example, or "What's the difference between a castle and a palace?") to more serious subjects that relate to the material being presented.

At various points, Kuplic asks a participant to select a balloon, pop it, read the slip of paper, and speak extemporaneously about the topic for two minutes. If the participant is completely befuddled, he or she has the option of coming back the following morning with a prepared five-minute report.

Over the course of the two weeks, each participant is selected to choose at least one balloon, and Kuplic says he makes the selection process as lighthearted as possible. He might take the last person back from a break, for example, or choose someone who yawns on the first day.

"It's important that participants don't see the balloons as a punishment. It's a way to have some fun during this long session," Kuplic says. "But extemporaneous speaking also helps hone communication skills. It helps people learn to think on their feet and can improve their self-confidence when they realize they can live through the exercise."

GAME #18: Phrase Craze

Game Categories:
- ☐ Opener
- ☐ Energizer
- ☐ Communication
- ☐ Team-building
- ☑ Review
- ☐ Topical

❖ **Purpose:** To lead a nontraditional review session and garner course feedback.

❖ **Time Required:** 10 minutes.

❖ **Size of Group:** Unlimited.

❖ **Materials Required:** Paper and writing utensils for all participants.

❖ **The Exercise in Action:**
Julie Boyce, a self-employed trainer, consultant, and therapist in Springfield, MO, closes her sessions by listing several unfinished phrases—I learned..., I was surprised..., I understand...—on a flipchart, and asking each participant to choose and complete one of the sentences. After allowing two minutes for participants to write their answers, she asks them to share what they've written.

The exercise serves as a nice summary of key points, provides good facilitator feedback, and leaves participants with a positive feeling about what they have learned, Boyce says.

Categories:
- ☐ Opener
- ☐ Energizer
- ☑ Communication
- ☐ Team-building
- ☐ Review
- ☐ Topical

❖ **Purpose:** To demonstrate the importance of listening skills.

❖ **Time Required:** 10 minutes.

❖ **Size of Group:** Unlimited, but participants must work in pairs.

❖ **Materials Required:** Many sets of dominos; diagram prepared in advance by the trainer.

❖ **The Exercise in Action:** Shari Petrak, a liability claims training specialist, Nationwide Insurance, in Columbus, OH, pairs off participants and designates one person in each pair as the "sender" and the other as the "receiver."

The sender is given a diagram showing a configuration of 10 dominos. The receiver gets a matching set of dominos. A barrier such as a notebook is placed between the two. The sender's job is to verbally communicate the pattern shown on her diagram to the receiver, who tries to duplicate it. The sender is not permitted to see the receiver's work. Petrak allows six to eight minutes for the exercise, depending on the complexity of the arrangements.

She follows up with a discussion of barriers to clear communication, such as using terms unfamiliar to the other person, giving instructions too rapidly, or failing to listen carefully to questions.

GAME #20: Customer Questions

Game	☐ Opener	☐ Team-building
Categories:	☐ Energizer	☑ Review
	☐ Communication	☑ Topical: Customer Service

❖ **Purpose:** To improve retention of new product information during customer service training.

❖ **Time Required:** 10 to 20 minutes.

❖ **Size of Group:** 8 to 16.

❖ **Materials Required:** Flashcards prepared in advance by the trainer.

❖ **The Exercise in Action:** Mastering a wide range of ever-changing product and service information is crucial for sales and service phone representatives who often spend a majority of their day responding to customer questions. Cindy Turbow, a trainer with Microsoft Corp. in Redmond, WA, uses flashcards in role-play situations.

The cards feature questions asked by customers, based on the company's call reports. Depending on the group's size, Turbow has participants either role play in pairs or role play as a group. As pairs, participants take turns playing the role of customer and service representative, posing questions written on the flashcards. Turbow says this gives them the opportunity to hear different jargon and terms customers might use, while finding answers to the questions.

As a group, Turbow assumes the role of customer and participants take turns being the representative. While Turbow role plays with one participant, others are asked to come up with correct answers as well.

Turbow says she finds the flashcards an invaluable resource since she no longer has to "come up with situation after situation on the spot."

Game Categories:
- ☐ Opener
- ☑ Energizer
- ☑ Communication
- ☐ Team-building
- ☐ Review
- ☐ Topical

❖ **Purpose:** To get participants actively involved in thinking creatively and following directions.

❖ **Time Required:** 10 minutes.

❖ **Size of Group:** Unlimited.

❖ **Materials Required:** None.

❖ **The Exercise in Action:** For this exercise, Carly Murdy, a trainer with the UAW/GM Human Resource Center in Auburn Hills, MI, gives these precise instructions: "In the following line of letters, cross out six letters so that the remaining letters—without altering their sequence—spell a familiar English word." (Answer below.)

BSAINXLEATNTEARS

Answer: The solution is simple enough if you follow the directions to the letter (no pun intended): Cross out the letters in the sequence that spell "six letters," and you're left with the word "banana."

GAME #22: Building Blocks

Game Categories:

- ☐ Opener
- ☐ Energizer
- ☐ Communication
- ☐ Team-building
- ☑ Review
- ☐ Topical

❖ **Purpose:** To actively involve participants in a review session.

❖ **Time Required:** 20 minutes or longer, depending on amount of material to review.

❖ **Size of Group:** Unlimited. In a large group, participants might work in review teams of six or so.

❖ **Materials Required:** A set of children's building blocks.

❖ **The Exercise in Action:** Especially when particularly dry material is involved, trainer Sherri Williams livens up review sessions with rectangular building blocks. First she arranges the blocks in a tower by placing three side-by-side on a desk or table, then laying three more at right angles across those, and so on until all the blocks are used.

A player (or team) earns the right to take a block from any layer of the tower except the top one by correctly answering a review question. The game ends when the tower falls or when only one layer of blocks is left, whichever comes first. The player (or team) with the most blocks wins, as long as that player didn't topple the tower.

GAME #23: Curing the Nonverbal Blues

Game Categories:
- ☐ Opener
- ☑ Energizer
- ☑ Communication
- ☐ Team-building
- ☐ Review
- ☐ Topical

❖ **Purpose:** To illustrate the positive and negative effects of nonverbal communication.

❖ **Time Required:** 20 to 30 minutes.

❖ **Size of Group:** 8 to 15.

❖ **Materials Required:** Name tents prepared in advance by the trainer.

❖ **The Exercise in Action:** One or two days into a multi-day session, Becky Wedemeyer, director of human resources at Chesapeake Bay Seafood House Associates in Vienna, VA, writes a different emotion or personality trait on the inside of each participant's name tent (for example, excited, impatient, shy, bored, tired, inconvenienced, mad, happy, etc.). She then asks participants to stand up and act out their designated emotion for 5 to 10 seconds. While one participant "performs," the others are asked to jot down which emotion they think is being acted out and how they came to that conclusion.

After each participant has acted out an emotion, the class discusses results to see how many guessed correctly. Certain emotions are invariably mistaken for others—hurried/impatient/inconvenienced, or shy/disinterested, for example. Managers learn the importance of being more aware of the message they might be sending through their own body language.

To avoid putting people on the spot, Wedemeyer attempts to assign the easiest emotions to portray (happy/sad) to those who've proven more reserved throughout the session, and leaves the tougher, more subtle emotions to those she thinks won't embarrass as easily.

She also suggests that participants might find it helpful to pretend they're performing a job function in which the emotion is common.

GAME #24: Hopping Down the Bunny Trail

❖ **Purpose:** To make review sessions more fun by using a colorful prop.

❖ **Time Required:** As long as 30 minutes, depending on the amount of material to review.

❖ **Size of Group:** 10 to 20.

❖ **Materials Required:** As many plastic Easter eggs as participants. Numbered slips of paper prepared by the trainer.

❖ **The Exercise in Action:** Plastic, colored Easter eggs are used to make review more fun in Ann Hensel's courses.

Hensel, an instructor at Discover Card Services, Inc., Columbus, OH, asks each participant, near the end of the session, to compile a list of four or five questions and answers related to the course material, using notes or other resources.

She inserts slips of paper numbered according to class size—for example 1 through 15 in a class of 15 participants—inside the eggs, and gives each participant an egg. She has an equal number of small prizes, numbered correspondingly.

She asks participants to sit in a circle, and one person is selected to begin the review by tossing an egg to someone else. The person who throws the egg then asks a question. If the recipient answers correctly, he or she keeps the egg that was thrown, tosses the egg to another person, and asks a different question. If, however, a participant fails to answer correctly, the egg is tossed back to its original owner, who throws it to someone else and asks the same question.

When everyone—time permitting—has had a chance to participate, Hensel stops the game, has participants open their eggs, and gives them the numbered prizes that match the numbers they find in the eggs.

Participants enjoy the method more than a traditional question-and-answer session, Hensel says, and also benefit from formulating their own questions. The instructor, in turn, gets a chance to observe rather than facilitate.

GAME #25: The Fishbowl

Game Categories:
- ☐ Opener
- ☐ Energizer
- ☐ Communication
- ☐ Team-building
- ☐ Review
- ☑ Topical: Diversity

❖ **Purpose:** To help participants see the diversity issue from "both sides of the fishbowl."

❖ **Time Required:** 20 to 30 minutes.

❖ **Size of Group:** Unlimited.

❖ **Materials Required:** None.

❖ **The Exercise in Action:** This simple "fishbowl" activity spurs interaction and discussion among participants about discrimination, and works well as a lead-in for methods to address diversity among co-workers, according to Nancy Reece. Reece, associate executive director at the YMCA, Kankakee, IL, credits the idea to Everett Christmas, national field consultant for YMCA USA.

Reece begins with a discussion on discrimination, using comparisons such as left-handed people versus right-handed people, and short people versus tall people. She gives the group some interesting statistics on what makes the two groups unique. For example, "Did you know that left-handers live four years less on average than right-handers?" She then divides the class into lefties and righties and asks the majority group (in this example, the righties) to form a circle around the minority group. She gives the inner circle five minutes to discuss their experiences *as* left-handers, while the outer circle discusses their experiences *with* left-handers. There is no interaction between groups. After the activity, Reece debriefs by discussing each group's experiences.

She does the activity again, this time with the class divided into two groups based on more potentially controversial differences, such as men and women, black and white, overweight and thin. She suggests choosing the topic based on the mix of the class so that participants have strong feelings about the group they choose. The inner circle, once again, discusses their experiences *as* the minority group, while the outer circle discusses their experiences *with* the minority group. Following the activity and debriefing, Reece introduces the skills that help participants deal more effectively with diversity on the job, including communication skills, appropriate ways to express opinions, and understanding diversity in the workplace.

GAME #26: Darting About

Game Categories:
☐ Opener   ☐ Team-building
☐ Energizer   ☑ Review
☐ Communication   ☐ Topical

❖ **Purpose:** To allow participants to determine the point values during your review games.

❖ **Time Required:** 25 minutes.

❖ **Size of Group:** 10 to 15.

❖ **Materials Required:** Children's dart board game.

❖ **The Exercise in Action:** A sticky combination of darts and baseball helps Alvin O'Neal get around an equally sticky (and common) problem many trainers have with prepared review games: participants might not always agree with the point values assigned to certain questions. How often have you read a question during a game and heard someone groan, "*That* was worth 100 points?"

O'Neal, national sales trainer for NightRider Overnite Copy Service, Houston, puts the onus of determining point values on *participants* by asking them to toss VELCRO™-covered balls at a baseball game board he purchased at a local toy store. Tossing the ball into the space marked "single" means the question is worth one point, a "double" is worth two points, and so on. The same principle can be applied to dart boards that use VELCRO™.

If nothing else, he says, have participants roll dice to determine each question's point value or put a deck of cards in a hat and ask participants to draw one before answering a question, with face cards worth 15 points and all others worth their face value. Participants still might good-naturedly complain about "easy" questions worth lots of points, but everyone knows they have the same chance to hit it big.

GAME #27: Brainstorming Bonanza

Game Categories:
- ☐ Opener
- ☑ Energizer
- ☐ Communication
- ☐ Team-building
- ☐ Review
- ☐ Topical

❖ **Purpose:** To energize the group by generating a lot of ideas quickly in a brainstorming session and reducing participant resistance.

❖ **Time Required:** 20 minutes.

❖ **Size of Group:** 8 to 10.

❖ **Materials Required:** Flipchart pages; different colored markers; a music selection (CD or tape) and a player.

❖ **The Exercise in Action:** Gail Estes, training advisor for the human resources department at Mobil Oil Corp., Fairfax, VA, first chooses a topic relevant to the course to brainstorm. For example, in a course on improving customer service, she chooses "Buying Experiences" as the topic. She writes three to five questions pertaining to the topic, one question per flipchart page, and then posts the pages on the walls around the room. Questions may include, for example, "What would you describe as your best buying experience?" "What would you describe as your worst buying experience?" "What would you describe as an ideal buying experience?"

Depending on the number of participants, Estes has more than one flipchart page with the same question. With larger groups, she splits the participants into two groups and puts them in separate rooms.

She then gives each participant a different colored marker (that matches the color of his or her name tag) and asks everyone to stand at a flipchart. She tells them to write as many ideas as they can about the question while she plays recorded music. Participants cannot repeat ideas already listed. When the music stops, participants move to the next flipchart. After 10 to 15 minutes, Estes stops the activity and counts up the ideas each participant wrote. She rewards the person with the most ideas with a prize, and smaller prizes for the other participants. The exercise usually generates 150 to 200 ideas.

Estes says the light competition spurs participants to write as many ideas as possible, whereas in typical groups, ideas dead-end, reducing spontaneity and wasting time.

GAME #28: Slogans

Game Categories:
- ☑ Opener
- ☑ Energizer
- ☐ Communication
- ☐ Team-building
- ☐ Review
- ☐ Topical

❖ **Purpose:** To spark creative thinking skills at the outset (or at any point) of a training session.

❖ **Time Required:** 10 minutes.

❖ **Size of Group:** Unlimited, but participants should work in small groups of three to six.

❖ **Materials Required:** Writing materials for each participant.

❖ **The Exercise in Action:** Curt Hale opens his sessions by asking each person to write a company slogan, omitting the company name: For example, Chevrolet's "The Heartbeat of America," Charmin's "Squeezably soft," and Burger King's "Have it your way." Hale writes the slogans on flipchart pages. He then breaks the class into groups and has each group try to match the correct company name to each slogan. Results are tallied to see which group got the most correct answers.

Hale, a quality improvement manager for General Mills, Cedar Rapids, IA, then leads a discussion of what the slogans say about the companies they represent and has groups spend five minutes thinking of slogans that represent their own company's purpose and values.

GAME #29: Step by Step

Game Categories:
☐ Opener ☐ Team-building
☐ Energizer ☑ Review
☐ Communication ☐ Topical

❖ **Purpose:** To help participants review the elements of a multi-step process.

❖ **Time Required:** 20 minutes.

❖ **Size of Group:** Unlimited, but participants should work in an even number of small groups.

❖ **Materials Required:** Construction paper.

❖ **The Exercise in Action:** David Plantier says illustrations are an effective review tool in classes where participants must learn multi-step sequences, and there's a simple, cost-effective way to get those illustrations: Have participants create them.

Here's how the exercise works: Plantier, president of Boiler & Combustion Seminars in Bloomington, MN, breaks the class into an even number of small groups and asks each group to draw the steps of the process on separate pieces of construction paper. If there are more steps than group members, some participants must do more than one drawing. He gives each group four minutes to complete their drawings. Only pictures are allowed, no words can be used.

Plantier then pairs each small group with an "opponent" group and has the groups stand and face each other in a line. One group shows its drawings out of order while the other group shuffles those holding the pictures until all of the steps are in the correct sequence. If a group didn't complete all of the drawings (only five of a six-step process, for example) the opposite group must still put the five steps in order and then identify the missing step. He then has the groups switch opponents and repeat the exercise.

GAME #30: To Build a Car

Game Categories:

- ☐ Opener
- ☐ Energizer
- ☐ Communication
- ☑ Team-building
- ☐ Review
- ☐ Topical

❖ **Purpose:** To help group members better understand the value of one another's contributions.

❖ **Time Required:** 20 to 30 minutes.

❖ **Size of Group:** Unlimited, but participants should work in small groups of four to six.

❖ **Materials Required:** Flipchart paper for each small group; markers for each small group.

❖ **The Exercise in Action:** David Moorefield begins his car-building exercise by breaking the class into groups of four to six, and giving each group a sheet of flipchart paper and some markers. Each group is instructed to draw the outline of a car on the paper. (To save time, the instructor may prepare the drawings in advance.)

Each member adds one detail to the drawing, to illustrate a strength he or she brings to the group, and labels the relationship. For example, a participant might draw a headlight and write beside it, "I provide long-range vision."

The groups have 15 minutes to complete their cars, after which they take turns explaining their drawings to the class. Each member describes his or her own addition to the car.

The method is good for helping new team members learn one another's strengths, says Moorefield, a training specialist at EDS, Plano, TX. It also helps established teams gain an awareness of what various members contribute.

GAME #31: Small Group Leaders

Game Categories:
- ☐ Opener
- ☑ Energizer
- ☐ Communication
- ☐ Team-building
- ☐ Review
- ☐ Topical

❖ **Purpose:** To creatively "select" small group leaders.

❖ **Time Required:** 2 minutes.

❖ **Size of Group:** Unlimited.

❖ **Materials Required:** None.

❖ **The Exercise in Action:** Selecting volunteers or assigning leaders for small-group activities is painless and enjoyable with these ideas, says Barbara Peterson, a manager for U.S. West, Minneapolis:

- Ask participants to tally the number of anatomical feet they have in their household (four for a cat, two for a child, and so on). The person in each group with the highest score is the "volunteer" leader.

- Ask everyone to write their middle names on a sheet of paper. The member of each group with the longest middle name is the leader.

- Ask people their mothers' first names. The person in each set whose mother's first name is last alphabetically is chosen.

Peterson also offers a tip for splitting up people who are familiar to the presenter as "problem" participants—perhaps because they talk or make annoying comments during presentations—provided the instructor has access to telephone numbers, birth dates, or other numerical data.

Add up the digits, for example, in the telephone numbers of the difficult participants before class or during a break. Find a pattern that will divide the problem people. For example, ask everyone with an even total $(4+1+3+5+2+7+8+3+6+3 = 42)$ to sit on one side of the room, odd on the other. Or simply divide them by the last digit in their phone numbers. The planned separation is transparent to the intended targets. This method is useful for mixing groups even if no such difficulties exist.

GAME #32: Story Time

**Game
Categories:**
☐ Opener
☐ Energizer
☐ Communication
☐ Team-building
☑ Review
☐ Topical

❖ **Purpose:** To encourage creative thinking during review sessions.

❖ **Time Required:** 30 minutes.

❖ **Size of Group:** Unlimited.

❖ **Materials Required:** Name tents prepared in advance by the trainer.

❖ **The Exercise in Action:** Prior to class, Frederick Faiks writes two words on the inside of participants' tented name cards. When it's time to review course topics, he has participants turn their tags inside out to reveal the words. He then begins narrating a story related to the course theme, and passes the story off to a participant, who must continue it while weaving in one of her two random words before passing the story off to another participant. (Example: "It is 2001 and I walked into my office. It is not at all like it was in 1995. One primary difference is…" and a participant would use one of her words in a phrase to complete the sentence.)

The story goes around the room twice until all the random words are used. "The brain will try to connect any dissimilar concepts if it is instructed to do so, and some interesting solutions evolve," says Faiks, a research engineer at Steelcase, Inc., in Grand Rapids, MI. "It's also a lot of fun and reinforces learning."

GAME #33: The Outcast

Game Categories:
- ☐ Opener
- ☐ Energizer
- ☐ Communication
- ☐ Team-building
- ☐ Review
- ☑ Topical: Diversity

❖ **Purpose:** To raise awareness and release tension early in the session.

❖ **Time Required:** 20 minutes.

❖ **Size of Group:** Unlimited, but participants should work in small groups of three to five.

❖ **Materials Required:** None.

❖ **The Exercise in Action:** Steven Boyington, a training specialist with American Express TCG, Salt Lake City, first divides the class into small groups of three to five participants and has them list 10 "subgroups" that constitute a diverse workforce. Boyington creates a master list of categories by circulating among the groups. Some examples include: race, gender, sexual orientation, age, physical disabilities, economic status, language, etc. He asks participants to list all the categories in which they currently fall or have belonged to at some time in their lives. Boyington then asks for volunteers to share categories to which they belong.

Next, he asks participants to pick one category where they felt the most like an "outcast" or when they "just didn't fit in" and to share their individual experiences with the class. Responses include things like: being the last one chosen on an athletic team, coming from the only Jewish family in the community, feeling like the poorest kid in school, or always being the tallest girl in class. Boyington says participants discover that without exception, everyone at some point has felt what it's like to be different (diverse).

GAME #34: Looking for a Leader

Game Categories:
- ☑ Opener
- ☐ Energizer
- ☐ Communication
- ☐ Team-building
- ☐ Review
- ☐ Topical

❖ **Purpose:** To break the ice and show participants how leadership can affect an entire organization.

❖ **Time Required:** 10 minutes.

❖ **Size of Group:** Unlimited.

❖ **Materials Required:** None.

❖ **The Exercise in Action:** Larry Cox, manager of training and development, CSX Transportation, Jacksonville, FL, presents this scenario to small groups at the outset of a session: The president of our company has just resigned, and we're looking for a new leader. We have received several inquiries from people interested in the position, and the class has been chosen to determine which person should have the job.

Cox then gives one name to each group that he's prepared in advance and tells them to come up with five actions or steps the group feels that person would take to bring the company more in line with his or her personality and what it would mean to the firm. Some of the names he has assigned to small groups include Madonna, Dr. Ruth, Elvis, Jimmie Swaggart, Walt Disney, Oprah. Once the groups finish, each presents its findings to the entire class, which then selects a "new" president from the candidates.

GAME #35: Cartoon Captions

Game Categories:
- ☐ Opener
- ☑ Energizer
- ☐ Communication
- ☐ Team-building
- ☐ Review
- ☐ Topical

❖ **Purpose:** To add levity to otherwise dry subject matter.

❖ **Time Required:** 10 minutes.

❖ **Size of Group:** Unlimited.

❖ **Materials Required:** Cartoons relating to the course topic.

❖ **The Exercise in Action:** Topical cartoons—minus their captions—can add levity to dry subject matter, says Mark Poore, a training coordinator at Precision Computer Systems, Inc., Sioux Falls, SD.

Poore displays cartoons relating to specific courses on an overhead projector. Before revealing their captions, he solicits ideas for substitute captions from the group. These are often funnier than the original punchlines, he says.

GAME #36: Best Guess

Game Categories:
- ☐ Opener
- ☑ Energizer
- ☐ Communication
- ☐ Team-building
- ☐ Review
- ☐ Topical

❖ **Purpose:** To introduce participants to unfamiliar and obscure terms to be taught later in the course.

❖ **Time Required:** 10 to 30 minutes.

❖ **Size of Group:** Unlimited, but participants should be broken into small groups of four to eight.

❖ **Materials Required:** Writing paper for everyone in the group; index cards, prepared in advance by the trainer.

❖ **The Exercise in Action:** Mike Amos, vice president of Sandia Holdings, Inc., in Phoenix, AZ, uses a variation on the game "Dictionary" as an energizer in his training sessions. He breaks participants into groups and provides them with unfamiliar and obscure terms he's going to cover later in the class.

Group members are asked to write their "best guess" definitions of the words on slips of paper. The slips of paper are then thrown into a hat, and the correct definition is slipped in with those guesses. One group member reads aloud each definition, as others vote on which they think is correct. Participants who get peers to vote for their "imposter" definitions receive points, as do the people who select the "right" definition. Individuals with the most points in each group receive a prize.

GAME #37: First Impressions

Game Categories:
- ☑ Opener
- ☐ Energizer
- ☐ Communication
- ☐ Team-building
- ☐ Review
- ☐ Topical

❖ **Purpose:** To help participants get to know their classmates while learning something about first impressions and preconceptions.

❖ **Time Required:** 10 minutes.

❖ **Size of Group:** Unlimited, but participants should work in small groups of three.

❖ **Materials Required:** Two forms, prepared in advance by the trainer.

❖ **The Exercise in Action:** Drake Beil, president of Solutions, Inc., Honolulu, begins this exercise by dividing the group into triads. Each person is given two identical forms. They may be on the top and bottom halves of the same page to save paper. Each contains five blanks, labeled with queries about personal tastes, such as "favorite TV show," "perfect vacation," or "favorite food." Topics can vary, from nonsensical to job-related, as desired.

Participants fill out one such sheet for each of the other two members of their trios, guessing at what they think the others' tastes might be. Guessing is essential, so only two or three minutes are allowed to fill in the blanks.

Once completed, participants give the sheets to the people to whom they refer. The discussion that follows focuses on what the guesses were based on, whether any were correct, and whether two people guessed the same thing about one participant.

Says Beil: "People talk, find out about each other, laugh, scream, and have a lot of fun." The instructor can leave it at that, as a great way for people to make friends in a class full of strangers, or use the exercise as a lead-in for a discussion of diversity and the risk of making uninformed assumptions about people.

GAME #38: The Rating Game

Game Categories:
- ☐ Opener
- ☑ Energizer
- ☐ Communication
- ☐ Team-building
- ☑ Review
- ☐ Topical

❖ **Purpose:** To energize a group after a lunch break and serve as a mini-review.

❖ **Time Required:** 15 minutes.

❖ **Size of Group:** 15 to 20, and group should be broken into three small groups.

❖ **Materials Required:** Writing paper.

❖ **The Exercise in Action:** Willy Ashbrook, national sales manager for Deluxe Sales Development Systems in Lakewood, CO, uses this group review technique to get things moving after lunch or at the beginning of the second day of a session:

- Break participants into three groups.

- Ask each group to formulate two questions pertaining to materials covered. They may use textbooks, notes, flipchart pages on walls, or any other available resources.

- After questions are written, put away reference materials. The review is a "closed-book" exercise.

- Instruct Group A to ask Group B a question. Tell participants their group's answer should be as thorough as possible.

- Have Group C critique Group B's answer, using a 10-point scale. Ask Group C to explain how Group B's answer could have been improved to earn a top rating of 10.

- Allow Group B to pose a question for Group C to answer, then have Group A evaluate the response and provide guidance on how the answer could have been improved.

- Repeat the process until every group has asked one question of each of the other groups.

- Provide small rewards for members of the group with the highest total score, as determined by their peers.

GAME #39: Put a Lid on It

Game Categories:	☐ Opener	☑ Team-building
	☐ Energizer	☐ Review
	☐ Communication	☐ Topical

❖ **Purpose:** To sensitize participants to the impact of differing personalities on groups.

❖ **Time Required:** 10 minutes.

❖ **Size of Group:** Unlimited, but participants should work in small groups of four or five.

❖ **Materials Required:** Baseball caps, customized in advance by the trainer (number depends on size of group).

❖ **The Exercise in Action:** To teach participants the value of recognizing and addressing the sensitive issue of group dynamics in the workplace, Samantha Doly breaks the class into groups of four or five and assigns each a problem that must be solved by consensus. She tells the groups that while they work on the problem, she will place customized baseball caps on the heads of three participants in each group. The hats are labeled:

- Know It All—Ignore Me
- Expert—Listen to Me
- Insecure—Encourage Me

Doly, staff training officer for the AMP Society, Brisbane, Australia, then instructs group members to treat the people wearing the hats according to the labels, although each person wearing a cap is unaware of what the cap says.

When forced to deal with those dynamics, Doly says, groups rarely reach consensus within the 10-minute time limit she sets. The point of the exercise, she says, is to teach participants to constantly be on the lookout for differing personalities that might affect a group.

GAME #40: In the Beginning...

Game Categories:

- ☐ Opener
- ☐ Energizer
- ☐ Communication
- ☐ Team-building
- ☐ Review
- ☑ Topical: Orientation

❖ **Purpose:** To get new employees immediately involved and focused on orientation material.

❖ **Time Required:** About 2 minutes per participant.

❖ **Size of Group:** Unlimited.

❖ **Materials Required:** Index cards prepared in advance by the participant.

❖ **The Exercise in Action:** In new-employee orientation training, where employees often feel tentative about asking questions, Susan Partee, a training assistant with O'Reilly/Ozark Automotive in Springfield, MO, writes questions concerning class content on index cards, one question per card and one card per participant.

After class introductions she passes out the cards and explains that each participant is responsible for answering—in writing—the question on his or her assigned card, and assures everyone their question will be covered in class before they are called upon for an answer. Then, at 15- to 20-minute intervals, she asks who has question number one, etc., (questions pertain to areas just discussed) and the participant with that question reads it aloud and provides the answer.

Partee says the exercise also serves to capture the attention of participants waiting for an answer to their own most pressing questions.

GAME #41: Group Résumés

Game Categories:

☑ Opener   ☑ Team-building
☐ Energizer   ☐ Review
☐ Communication   ☐ Topical

❖ **Purpose:** To build a group's self-esteem and foster bonds among participants.

❖ **Time Required:** 15 minutes.

❖ **Size of Group:** Unlimited, but participants should work in small groups of at least six.

❖ **Materials Required:** Markers and flipchart paper for each participant.

❖ **The Exercise in Action:** Betty Hertz, a consultant for Windemere Consultants, Anchorage, AK, divides participants into groups of at least six and asks them to compose a "group résumé" to publicize the groups' talents and experiences. Hertz chooses a job for the groups to apply for, and gives each group markers and a sheet of flipchart paper to display their résumés.

She tells them to include data that sells the group as a whole, such as educational backgrounds, total years of professional experience, positions held, talents, major accomplishments, etc. Each group shares its résumé, and the class celebrates the resources of the entire group.

GAME #42: Lottery Fever

Game Categories:
- ☐ Opener
- ☐ Energizer
- ☐ Communication
- ☐ Team-building
- ☑ Review
- ☐ Topical

❖ **Purpose:** To introduce a spirit of chance into review games.

❖ **Time Required:** 20 minutes.

❖ **Size of Group:** Unlimited.

❖ **Materials Required:** Lottery tickets (index cards), prepared in advance by the trainer.

❖ **The Exercise in Action:** Kaye Sanders, training coordinator with the Jacksonville Electric Authority, Jacksonville, FL, includes one of her self-designed lottery tickets in each packet of course materials, or simply tapes a ticket to every desk or chair. A corresponding number to each of the tickets is included in Sanders' large "lottery box."

At review time, Sanders asks each participant to write three or four review questions. She then selects a lottery number from the box and asks the person holding that ticket to answer a question relating to the course material. If he or she needs help, Sanders encourages the group to provide assistance.

Once the question is answered correctly, the person initially selected picks a number from the box and poses a question from his or her list. The lottery continues until everyone in the group has a chance to ask and answer a question. Sanders says participants should also prepare a list of questions in case someone says, "All the questions on my list have been asked."

GAME #43: Nickel Auction

Game Categories:
☐ Opener ☐ Energizer ☐ Communication

☑ Team-building ☐ Review ☐ Topical

❖ **Purpose:** To show how collaboration is often triumphant over competition.

❖ **Time Required:** 20 to 30 minutes.

❖ **Size of Group:** Unlimited, but group should be broken into five small groups.

❖ **Materials Required:** 10 nickels; 5 chairs.

❖ **The Exercise in Action:** Lisa Schreiber, president of Novations in Omaha, NE, uses this exercise to help participants explore alternatives to this common workplace problem:

lack of communication + uncertainty + perceived competition = irrational behavior

Called "nickel auction," the exercise requires 10 nickels, and starts with five chairs placed at the front of the classroom. Divide the large group into five smaller groups. Ask each group to pool their available pocket change and give it to a designated group representative. Have those five representatives come to the front of the room to sit with the other group representatives.

Then start your nickel auction. In round one, ask each representative—one by one—to bid or pass on one of the five nickels. Each nickel goes to the highest bidder, and bidding continues until all five nickels are gone. Send the representatives back to their groups with the remaining change. Review which groups won bidding contests and how much they paid for each nickel. (In Schreiber's class, winning bidders have paid as much as $4 for a nickel.)

Have groups pick new representatives for round two. But this time let the representatives have a private discussion together for five minutes. They inevitably decide to each bid one cent for each nickel and allow everyone to get one.

Schreiber again emphasizes how up-front collaboration and communication—rather than competition—sometimes mean all parties can go away feeling satisfied.

GAME #44: Hollywood Squares

Game Categories:	☐ Opener	☐ Team-building
	☐ Energizer	☑ Review
	☐ Communication	☐ Topical

❖ **Purpose:** To add a familiar sense of competition to review sessions in multi-day courses.

❖ **Time Required:** 15 minutes on each day after the first day's session.

❖ **Size of Group:** Unlimited.

❖ **Materials Required:** Prepared question cards; masking tape.

❖ **The Exercise in Action:** Kathleen Burke-Scheffler, a trainer with U.S. West in Minneapolis, says this review game works well in multiple-day training sessions. At the end of the first day of class, she has each participant write two or three questions derived from the day's content. Questions can be in multiple choice, true/false, or fill-in-the-blank formats. She collects the questions and, if necessary, adds a few of her own.

At the beginning of day two, she uses the questions for a takeoff on "Hollywood Squares." She simulates the tic-tac-toe game show format by setting up three chairs at the front of the class, asking three volunteers to sit on the floor in front of them, three to sit in the chairs, and three to stand behind them.

Each of the nine "celebrities" is given a card with an "X" printed on one side and an "O" on the other to tape to their bodies as questions are successfully answered.

She then asks for two volunteers to serve as contestants. The contestants pick members of the "celebrity" squares to answer the game's questions. She asks the contestants questions in turns. The contestants respond with "agree" or "disagree" to the panel's response as they try to form a tic-tac-toe.

Remaining participants not involved in the game are given cards that say agree on one side and disagree on the other to flash to contestants to aid in their decision making.

GAME #45: Positive Visualization

Game	☑ Opener	☐ Team-building
Categories:	☐ Energizer	☐ Review
	☐ Communication	☐ Topical

❖ **Purpose:** To show participants the power of "positive visualization."

❖ **Time Required:** 15 minutes.

❖ **Size of Group:** Unlimited.

❖ **Materials Required:** A 10-inch piece of string; a washer of any size; paper.

❖ **The Exercise in Action:** Mark Evans, division training manager for Johnson Wax in Columbia, MD, often uses this opener to show participants how positive thinking can help them overcome stressful events in their professional lives, such as downsizings or ever-expanding job descriptions.

He first suggests that they all have the ability to assimilate any change through the use of positive thinking. "I tell them their minds cannot tell the difference between a real and imagined experience," he says. He also tells participants, "If you think the way you always think, you will get exactly what you've always gotten."

At this point there are always a few skeptics, so Evans says he'll "prove" the power of positive visualization with a demonstration. Participants are given a prop—a 10-inch piece of string with a washer attached to one end of it—and are asked to draw a circle on a piece of paper, placing arrows through the circle pointing north, south, east, and west.

He then gives groups these instructions:

1. Hold the washer/string one inch above the center of the circle, like a pendulum.

2. Close your eyes and think of the string moving from left to right with the weight acting as a pendulum—but don't move your hand.

3. Concentrate and visualize it in your mind and tell yourself it will happen automatically.

After a few seconds of deep concentration, have participants open their eyes and—in most cases—they'll see the weight move from left to right without their hand moving. Then Evans challenges them to make the weight move in other directions.

GAME #46: Get One/Give One

Game Categories:
- ☐ Opener
- ☐ Energizer
- ☐ Communication
- ☐ Team-building
- ☑ Review
- ☐ Topical

◆ **Purpose:** To creatively engage participants in a review session.

◆ **Time Required:** 15 minutes.

◆ **Size of Group:** 15 to 20.

◆ **Materials Required:** Pen and paper for everyone.

◆ **The Exercise in Action:** "Get one/Give one" is an engaging and effective end-of-the-day review, says Bonnie Plummer, executive director of Capital Sierra Administrative Training Center, Sacramento, CA.

She asks the participants to independently list important ideas or actions they pick up during the training day, then take those sheets across the room to an unfamiliar participant and compare notes. Participants add one item to their lists from their partner's brainstorm pages, and should remain standing and change partners every two to three minutes. Plummer sometimes uses music, dance steps, and hand motions as people move throughout the room.

GAME #47: The Paper Cup

Game Categories:

- ☐ Opener
- ☑ Energizer
- ☐ Communication
- ☑ Team-building
- ☐ Review
- ☐ Topical

❖ **Purpose:** To quickly demonstrate to participants how teamwork can improve brainstorming sessions.

❖ **Time Required:** 10 minutes.

❖ **Size of Group:** Unlimited.

❖ **Materials Required:** A paper cup.

❖ **The Exercise in Action:** This simple exercise, suggested by Dan Griep, a plant manager of Ramaley Printing in St. Paul, MN, uses a single paper cup as a prop.

Griep first asks everyone to think of as many uses for a paper cup as they can in 30 seconds. Most individuals will come up with four to six uses. Next, he has participants form small groups of two or three and gives them 30 seconds to think of uses for the paper cup. They can usually think of 9 to 11 uses. Finally, Griep chooses several participants to write on flipchart pages all the ideas the entire group throws out in 30 seconds. The group together will typically come up with 20 to 30 uses.

GAME #48: The Power of Imagination

Game Categories:
- ☐ Opener
- ☑ Energizer
- ☐ Communication
- ☐ Team-building
- ☐ Review
- ☐ Topical

❖ **Purpose:** To stimulate discussion on the importance of perspective.

❖ **Time Required:** 20 minutes.

❖ **Size of Group:** Unlimited.

❖ **Materials Required:** Poster-sized blowups of unique photos, prepared in advance by the trainer.

❖ **The Exercise in Action:** Calling his activity the "Power of Imagination," Don Allison, national sales trainer for Hallmark Cards, Kansas City, uses photo blowups to illustrate how using unique ideas or techniques can make basic information more interesting.

The photos are taken at angles that make identifying the objects difficult. The objects are "blown up" larger than life, or show a closeup of only a small part of the subject. Allison's blowups include a donut, a turtle shell, an alligator snout, a piece of grass sticking up out of the snow, a portion of hair on the back of someone's head, and the closure at the top of a purse. Can you guess the example shown above? (The answer is listed below.)

He hangs 20 of the posters in the meeting room and asks participants to try to describe on an entry form what each poster is. The reward for getting the most correct answers is a dinner for two (you may choose some other appropriate reward).

Answer: Eyeglasses

GAME #49: Close Enough?

Game Categories:
- ☐ Opener
- ☐ Energizer
- ☑ Communication
- ☑ Team-building
- ☑ Review
- ☐ Topical

❖ **Purpose:** To show groups the need to carefully discuss *all* of the answers before choosing which is correct.

❖ **Time Required:** 10 minutes.

❖ **Size of Group:** Unlimited.

❖ **Materials Required:** One quiz per group, prepared in advance by trainer.

❖ **The Exercise in Action:** A quiz with one correct answer and three very close answers for each question, serves as an effective review for Mark Hinkel of the Congregational Bible Church, Marietta, GA.

Hinkel breaks the class into groups and passes out one quiz per group. On each quiz, a single question is marked for that group to answer. Each group chooses the answer it believes is correct, and with Hinkel serving as a facilitator, discusses its choice with the class. Participation is usually excellent, Hinkel says, because groups carefully discuss *all* the answers before choosing which is correct.

GAME #50: The Art of Self-Review

Game Categories:

- ☐ Opener
- ☐ Energizer
- ☐ Communication
- ☐ Team-building
- ☑ Review
- ☐ Topical

❖ **Purpose:** To lead participants through a self-review session.

❖ **Time Required:** 5 to 10 minutes.

❖ **Size of Group:** Unlimited.

❖ **Materials Required:** None.

❖ **The Exercise in Action:** An hour or so into a session, Robert Schwarz, a professional trainer with the International Association of Lions Clubs, Oak Brook, IL, divides learners into pairs for a self-review process. One member of each duo is instructed to pretend that the other has just arrived and needs help in catching up with what was missed. The first person takes five minutes to update the "latecomer" on everything covered thus far and how it can be applied to his or her work. When the person providing the review is through, the listener steps out of character and states any important information that was missed.

Says Schwarz: "Requiring each participant to articulate what he or she has learned not only enhances memory but greatly reduces my burden to periodically review and consolidate, which is now done more meaningfully by each individual." The exercise, if done occasionally throughout the day, makes an end-of-day review unnecessary, Schwarz says.

GAME #51: Able to Leap Straw Buildings...

Game Categories:

- ☐ Opener
- ☑ Energizer
- ☐ Communication
- ☑ Team-building
- ☐ Review
- ☐ Topical

❖ **Purpose:** To engage teams in a creative problem-solving exercise.

❖ **Time Required:** 15 minutes.

❖ **Size of Group:** Unlimited, but participants should work in pairs.

❖ **Materials Required:** A *bunch* of plastic drinking straws and many rolls of masking tape.

❖ **The Exercise in Action:** Straws and masking tape are the only tools needed for this team-building exercise used by Rocio Escobar, an instructor for Baskin-Robbins in Burbank, CA.

Escobar divides the class into teams and asks them to build a free-standing structure by taping straws together, but *not* taping anything to the floor, ceiling, or walls. Participants are timed, and the team with the tallest structure gets a prize.

GAME #52: Tag-Team Role-Playing

Game Categories:
- ☐ Opener
- ☐ Energizer
- ☐ Communication
- ☑ Team-building
- ☐ Review
- ☐ Topical

❖ **Purpose:** To instill a sense of teamwork during role plays as well as ease participant anxiety and remove the individual spotlight.

❖ **Time Required:** 20 minutes.

❖ **Size of Group:** Unlimited, but participants should work in pairs.

❖ **Materials Required:** Role-play questions and situations, prepared in advance by the trainer.

❖ **The Exercise in Action:** Participants who have never been involved in role-play exercises can be intimidated by the process. Lynne Guthrie places them in teams and uses a "tag team" approach to foster a sense of teamwork and reduce the fear level.

For example, to master the process of fact-finding or uncovering customer needs, sales trainees need to practice skills that include asking open- and closed-ended questions, listening, paraphrasing, and summarizing what a customer or sales prospect says. Guthrie splits participants into "Group A" to role play as sales representatives and "Group B" to pose as hypothetical customers. The customer group is given a detailed set of facts and needs about their business; the sales representative group is given sketchy information to prepare questions for the customer group. Prior to role plays, groups decide who will ask what types of questions, who will start the questioning, who will finish, and so on.

Guthrie, a training manager with Tele Direct Publications LTD in Scarsborough, Ontario, says the objective is for the sales representative group to uncover as many of the customer's business needs as possible using a "tag team" approach. For example, a member of the sales group asks a few questions of the customer group, then "tags" another group member if the line of questioning dead-ends or hits a snag, hoping the teammate can pick up the slack. Questioning continues this way until the group feels all customer needs have been answered. The customer group uses a similar tag-team process in answering questions.

GAME #53: The Technique Bank

Game Categories:

☑ Opener   ☐ Team-building
☑ Energizer   ☐ Review
☐ Communication   ☐ Topical

❖ **Purpose:** To get participants thinking about a session topic even before class begins.

❖ **Time Required:** 5 minutes at outset, then an ongoing process during the course.

❖ **Size of Group:** Unlimited.

❖ **Materials Required:** Post-It Notes (supplied by participants).

❖ **The Exercise in Action:** John Kane, manager of training and development at Traco Co., in Warrendale, PA, leads all registered participants through a "pre-session discovery" shortly before class begins. Kane asks them to write on two separate Post-It Notes two ideas related to the class topic that they feel would be of most benefit to other participants (for example, favorite time-management techniques for a course dealing with that subject).

When participants arrive at class, they take those two notes and stick them on a flipchart page labeled "The Technique Bank." Those notes are used later as a bank to "withdraw" techniques should participants get stumped in their own group discussions about the course's topic.

Kane calls the exercise a great "leveler," since all participants contribute regardless of experience. He says it's also a good mid-course energizer because it forces physical movement, which breaks preoccupation.

GAME #54: Distorted Messages

Game Categories:
- ☐ Opener
- ☐ Energizer
- ☑ Communication
- ☐ Team-building
- ☐ Review
- ☐ Topical

❖ **Purpose:** To illustrate how messages can be distorted through faulty communication, poor listening skills, or incomplete note taking.

❖ **Time Required:** 15 minutes.

❖ **Size of Group:** Unlimited, but participants should work in small groups of 5 to 10.

❖ **Materials Required:** Flipchart.

❖ **The Exercise in Action:** Clear communication relies on good listening skills and note taking. Brenda Sara, a food and beverage trainer with Prime Hospitality Corp. in Fairfield, NJ, uses the following exercise, a variation of the old party game, "telephone."

With participants in groups of 5 to 10, she concocts a detailed "message" for each group. Since her participants are in the hotel and restaurant business, the message simulates something commonly heard from customers in their jobs.

Example: "I'm calling to say that the Wakison party (or insert own customer name) will be coming on Thursday night at 7:00 instead of tonight at 8:30, and we will need two highchairs and a booster seat." All groups then form a circle, and the trainer communicates the message to the first participant on her left, who passes it on until every group member has heard it. The last participant to receive the message then writes it down on a flipchart.

When all are finished, Sara turns over a flipchart page with her original message so that groups can compare how distorted or accurate their final versions are.

Sara says names are frequently changed or times omitted in these final versions—mirroring an on-the-job problem. "We've had problems in our business where front-desk employees distort or don't write down a complete message, and communication is bungled, resulting in upset customers," Sara says. Participants are purposefully given no ground rules during the exercise—they aren't told they can't ask for a repeat, for example, and have no restrictions on taking notes—to gauge the initiative taken to accurately retain information. Following the exercise, Sara reaffirms that those retention tools are encouraged.

GAME #55: Toothpick Tales

Game Categories:
☑ Opener ☐ Team-building
☐ Energizer ☐ Review
☐ Communication ☐ Topical

❖ **Purpose:** To break the ice in a group while affirming participants' uniqueness and their common connections.

❖ **Time Required:** 10 minutes.

❖ **Size of Group:** Unlimited, but participants should work in small groups of three to five.

❖ **Materials Required:** Twelve toothpicks for each participant.

❖ **The Exercise in Action:** Peg Jacobsen, a partner in HRD Associates in Mequon, WI, divides her groups into subgroups, then gives each participant 12 toothpicks. She asks them to share something about themselves in the group (I have a cat... like to ski...) and give a toothpick to anyone with like interests, and take one from those who don't share the interest. She reshuffles groups after five minutes.

At the end of the ice breaker, toothpicks are tallied, and Jacobsen makes the point that everyone wins with shared information.

GAME #56: Division by Candy Bar

Game Categories:
- ☐ Opener
- ☑ Energizer
- ☐ Communication
- ☑ Team-building
- ☐ Review
- ☐ Topical

❖ **Purpose:** To encourage participants to meet more people and form small groups that *aren't* made up of their friends and acquaintances.

❖ **Time Required:** 5 minutes.

❖ **Size of Group:** Unlimited.

❖ **Materials Required:** An assortment of candy bars.

❖ **The Exercise in Action:** Meeting people is one of the greatest side benefits of a training session. Participants, however, tend to stick close to friends and acquaintances.

To get around that, Darlene Smith, a family home developer with the Casey Family Program, Baton Rouge, LA, places a bowl of miniature candy bars on each classroom table with instructions for each participant to take one. The number of candy choices is the same as the number of tables. If there are six tables, for example, there are six different types of candy bars in the mix.

After everyone has selected a treat, she asks participants to sort themselves according to the candy chosen—all Milky Ways in one group, all Butterfingers in another, and so on—and to sit with the others who chose likewise. (**Note:** It's important that the total number of any type of candy bar is not greater than the number of seats at a single table.)

GAME #57: What's My Line?

Game Categories:
☐ Opener   ☐ Team-building
☐ Energizer   ☐ Review
☐ Communication   ☐ Topical

❖ **Purpose:** To help break the ice during a two-day session with participants who *think* they know each other.

❖ **Time Required:** 15 minutes.

❖ **Size of Group:** Unlimited.

❖ **Materials Required:** Pen and paper for everyone.

❖ **The Exercise in Action:** Nancy Junion, director of education and development with BAICOP, Tempe, AZ, uses this ice breaker on the second morning of a two-day seminar.

She confidentially interviews two or three participants and asks them to complete the following sentences:

- I started in this business in…
- My first position was as a…
- The best thing about me as an employee is…
- One thing my peers don't know about me is…
- Boy, was my face red when…

Armed with the information, Junion plays a version of "What's My Line?" with the class. She reads each person's individual responses one by one, and asks the participants to guess who the mystery person might be. Incorrect guesses eliminate people from the game, but the first person with a correct answer wins a small prize. If the interviewee somehow "stumps" the group, he or she wins the prize.

GAME #58: Word Association

Game Categories:

- ☐ Opener
- ☐ Energizer
- ☐ Communication
- ☐ Team-building
- ☑ Review
- ☐ Topical

❖ **Purpose:** To challenge participants during review sessions to come up with phrases that rely on word association.

❖ **Time Required:** 20 to 30 minutes.

❖ **Size of Group:** Unlimited, but participants should work in small groups of three to seven.

❖ **Materials Required:** Pen and paper for the small groups.

❖ **The Exercise in Action:** "Word association reviews tend to have a fairly high retention rate," says John Addy, a trainer with Management Development Specialists, Halifax, England, "because people are coming up with phrases they are going to remember. It also serves as a confidence-builder for attendees, most of whom are pretty surprised by their creative potential."

Addy divides the class into small groups and asks each to prepare a list of 10 random nouns (combination words are also allowed, such as "oven mitts" or "floppy disk"). The groups then swap their word lists and Addy allows them 20 minutes to make an association between each word on the list and a key learning point from the class.

Often, Addy says, it takes a couple of examples from him to get the groups going. He offers the following as a good idea starter:

In a class on effective public speaking, the group might make an association between the skills they have learned and the word "sugar" by writing, "Sugar is sweet. Keep your audience sweet by preparing adequately, maintaining eye contact with everyone, and keeping to your stated time," or "Sugar is an additive sweetener. Visual aids can add something to a presentation, but overindulgence can be a recipe for indigestion," or "Sugar cubes are given to horses as a reward and an incentive. Reward participants by saying something useful, interesting, or thought-provoking, thus giving them an incentive to come again."

When the groups are finished, each must fully describe the associated principle to the entire class.

GAME #59: The "I" Exercise

Game Categories:
- ☐ Opener
- ☐ Energizer
- ☑ Communication
- ☐ Team-building
- ☐ Review
- ☐ Topical

❖ **Purpose:** To help participants get off their favorite subject—themselves—and listen to others.

❖ **Time Required:** 2 minutes.

❖ **Size of Group:** Unlimited.

❖ **Materials Required:** None.

❖ **The Exercise in Action:** Dan Sepe, a trainer with Solutions, Inc., Waipahu, HI, uses the "I" exercise in communication skills courses.

The exercise can be used with large or small groups and takes about two minutes. Sepe has all participants stand and gives them a topic to discuss with their peers for two minutes, such as the differences between being married versus single or the differences between men and women. However, throughout the conversation, they can't use the words "I," "me," or "my." If they use one of those words, they must sit down.

Sepe says that all or nearly all participants are seated before the two minutes are up. He says the exercise shows people how self-centered they can be during conversations. The only way to be successful in the exercise—and as a good listener—is to focus on the other person by using open-ended questions to encourage the other person to speak about their ideas.

GAME #60: 72 Seconds of Fun

Game Categories:	☑ Opener	☐ Team-building
	☐ Energizer	☐ Review
	☐ Communication	☐ Topical

❖ **Purpose:** To introduce participants to one another at the outset of class.

❖ **Time Required:** 72 seconds.

❖ **Size of Group:** Unlimited.

❖ **Materials Required:** None.

❖ **The Exercise In Action:** Seventy-two seconds is all participants get for introductions in courses led by Ann Verhaagen, sales trainer with Avon Products, Newark, DE.

After Verhaagen introduces herself, she tells participants they have 72 seconds to meet as many people as possible. She instructs them to tell others their name, where they live, and what company (or department) they are with. When time's up, the class reconvenes.

This exercise, she says, gets participants on their feet and immediately involved in meeting others.

GAME #61: Leaderless Success

Game Categories:
- ☐ Opener
- ☐ Energizer
- ☐ Communication
- ☑ Team-building
- ☐ Review
- ☐ Topical

❖ **Purpose:** To show teams they don't necessarily need a traditional leader to function effectively.

❖ **Time Required:** 10 minutes.

❖ **Size of Group:** 15 to 20.

❖ **Materials Required:** None.

❖ **The Exercise in Action:** When working with groups of at least 15 or 20 participants in her leadership and team-building training sessions, Lucia Shillito asks the entire group to "huddle" together in one corner of the room. She has them stand so that they can place a hand on the shoulder of another participant.

Together, she says, they represent one life form—an amoeba, for example. The only way the "amoeba" can move is by each participant releasing one person's shoulder and touching someone else's shoulder. Each person must keep moving in this way. The group's goal is to arrive at the other end of the room through some sort of fabricated passageway—a gauntlet formed by lined-up chairs, for instance, that is smaller than the width of the group.

Shillito, a trainer in the Australian Taxation Department, says no one person can "lead" the group—it must lead itself via coordinated teamwork.

GAME #62: A Lot of Hot Air

Game	☐ Opener	☑ Team-building
Categories:	☐ Energizer	☐ Review
	☑ Communication	☐ Topical

❖ **Purpose:** To use a common prop—balloons—to illustrate learning points about team-building and communication skills.

❖ **Time Required:** 15 minutes.

❖ **Size of Group:** Unlimited.

❖ **Materials Required:** A large supply of balloons of all sizes.

❖ **The Exercise in Action:** The "balloon metaphor" is a favorite closing exercise of Cher Holton, executive director for the Holton Consulting Group, Raleigh, NC. The activity closes out her team-building session on a high note, and ties together key concepts from the source. Holton uses the exercise with groups of all sizes. Here's how it works:

Holton distributes balloons to everyone and asks them to blow them up and tie knots in them. Their challenge, when she gives the word, is to form groups and begin batting the balloons into the air, keeping them all aloft. There's only one catch: participants may hit their own balloon only twice consecutively; they have to hit someone else's before hitting their own again. After about a minute, Holton stops the exercise, and the group discusses what happened.

Holton says the activity can be altered to fit specific topics. The following questions are examples of how she uses the activity to facilitate team-building.

"How are these balloons like the members of your team?" Responses typically include: full of hot air, different sizes/shapes/colors, up and down, hard to control, you lose some of them, takes work to keep them together, etc.

"Did all of the balloons stay up at the same rate?" The point here is that some balloons—just like some people—are easier to control and deal with than others.

"Can one person keep all of the balloons up alone?" Here Holton emphasizes that it takes teamwork. She points out that though the group tended to run into each other and step on one another's toes, nobody minded because everyone was focused on the balloons—the *group* goal.

GAME #63: Black Jack

Game Categories:
- ☐ Opener
- ☑ Energizer
- ☐ Communication
- ☐ Team-building
- ☐ Review
- ☐ Topical

❖ **Purpose:** To elicit answers from participants and encourage them to volunteer throughout the course.

❖ **Time Required:** An ongoing exercise.

❖ **Size of Group:** Unlimited.

❖ **Materials Required:** A deck of playing cards (perhaps two if the group is unusually large or the day is unusually active).

❖ **The Exercise in Action:** Participants can't help but get involved in "Black Jack" as played in courses led by Chris McCann, training coordinator with Nationwide Insurance Co., Wallingford, CT.

Each participant receives a playing card (to be kept face down) upon entering the classroom. When McCann asks for volunteers or asks a question, the participant who volunteers or answers receives another card (to be kept face up).

When several participants have a set of cards, McCann says, "Let's gamble!" She awards anyone with "Black Jack" (a face card and an ace) a prize. If the session involves a lot of questioning, she tallies the scores at the end of the day and awards the participant with the most "Black Jacks" a prize.

GAME #64: Ball Toss

Game Categories:
- ☑ Opener
- ☐ Energizer
- ☐ Communication
- ☐ Team-building
- ☐ Review
- ☐ Topical

❖ **Purpose:** To help participants learn one another's names.

❖ **Time Required:** 10 to 15 minutes.

❖ **Size of Group:** Unlimited.

❖ **Materials Required:** A tennis ball.

❖ **The Exercise in Action:** Members of a group learn one another's names quickly with this exercise, says Judy Clarke, a training officer for American Express, Australia.

Participants stand in a circle. The instructor states her name and tosses a tennis ball to one of the participants. That person, in turn, says his name and tosses the ball to another. This continues until everyone has tossed the ball several times.

Then the rules change. As players toss the ball, they say the recipients' names instead of their own. The game always provides a few laughs while helping participants and instructor alike learn participants' names.

GAME #65: The Prize Box

Game Categories:
- ☐ Opener
- ☑ Energizer
- ☐ Communication
- ☐ Team-building
- ☑ Review
- ☐ Topical

❖ **Purpose:** To add spice to session-ending reviews.

❖ **Time Required:** 10 to 20 minutes.

❖ **Size of Group:** Unlimited.

❖ **Materials Required:** Index cards; a shoe box to house review questions; small prizes, procured in advance by the trainer; a "prize box" to house the goodies.

❖ **The Exercise in Action:** Gary Thompson, a customer service representative for ADP Automotive Claims in Etobicoke, Ontario, Canada, uses this twist on review ideas:

At the end of a session, he asks individuals or groups to formulate questions based on material covered, then place those questions in a shoe box. He places a number of small prizes—pens, chocolates, magazines, and so on—equal to the number of questions in another box.

The prize box is passed around the room, and one participant draws a prize, shows it to the rest of the class, and announces that a right answer to the next question drawn will win that prize. The question box is then circulated, and the individual or group wishing to contend for that prize draws a question. If two groups or individuals want the same prize, they both draw questions, and the first with a correct answer wins. The review continues until all questions are exhausted.

GAME #66: Cartoon Drawing

Game Categories:
- ☐ Opener
- ☐ Energizer
- ☑ Communication
- ☐ Team-building
- ☐ Review
- ☐ Topical

❖ **Purpose:** To increase participants' awareness of how "simple" directions may not always be simple.

❖ **Time Required:** 10 minutes.

❖ **Size of Group:** Unlimited.

❖ **Materials Required:** A transparency, prepared in advance by the trainer.

❖ **The Exercise in Action:** Everyone assumes they're able to follow simple instructions, Cindy Love says, and many people become frustrated when others seem unable to do the same. Love, an education specialist with Orlando Regional Healthcare System, Orlando, FL, expands participants' appreciation of good communication skills with this exercise:

She places a transparency of a familiar cartoon character's face—Bugs Bunny, for example—on the overhead projector, but does not turn it on. She gives participants pencils and blank sheets of paper, and asks them to follow her instructions as closely as possible:

"Draw a circle. Inside that circle draw two smaller, side-by-side circles nearer the top than the bottom. Under each of the smaller circles, draw three lines extending outward until they are outside the original circle…" and so on.

After the entire picture has been described, Love turns on the projector and shows the participants the original design. The difference between their work and the actual cartoon character illustrates the importance of clear instructions *and* careful listening.

GAME #67: Different Characters

Game	☐ Opener	☐ Team-building
Categories:	☐ Energizer	☐ Review
	☐ Communication	☑ Topical: Diversity

❖ **Purpose:** To increase participants' awareness of what it's like to be treated stereotypically.

❖ **Time Required:** 15 to 20 minutes.

❖ **Size of Group:** Unlimited.

❖ **Materials Required:** "Character sheets," prepared in advance by the trainer.

❖ **The Exercise in Action:** In sessions dealing with human diversity, Alison Wyles, a trainer at State Bank Centre, Adelaide, Australia, uses the following exercise:

She asks for three volunteers who are willing to speak briefly in front of the class. She gives each a script to read and informs them that they will be asked to read it to the class momentarily. She instructs them to leave the room, briefly, while she explains the exercise to the rest of the group.

Wyles tells the others the characters represented are a criminal, a politician, and a comedian. She tells them to boo, jeer, clap, laugh, and generally overreact to the scripts as they are read. She tells them to pay special attention to the body language and behavior of each reader as he or she hears the stereotypical reaction to the character they represent.

Wyles asks the volunteers to return. She tells them that they now have different personalities and that the group will treat them accordingly as they read their scripts. The criminal's script includes a life history documenting crimes and jail time. The politician is provided with a campaign platform speech. The comedian has a list of jokes. Each, therefore, draws a very different reaction from the crowd.

After all three have read their scripts, Wyles debriefs the class by asking volunteers how they felt upon receiving the audience's reaction, and by asking the class what behavior was observed in the readers. She explains that, while exaggerated, the same feelings and reactions are present in real-world exchanges between people of varying backgrounds. The point, she says, is to raise participants' awareness of their own reactions to others.

GAME #68: Cultural Introductions

Game Categories:
- ☑ Opener
- ☐ Energizer
- ☐ Communication
- ☐ Team-building
- ☐ Review
- ☐ Topical

❖ **Purpose:** To help a trainer quickly assess the audience.

❖ **Time Required:** 5 minutes.

❖ **Size of Group:** Unlimited.

❖ **Materials Required:** None.

❖ **The Exercise in Action:** Bob Boser, a quality engineer with Eastman Kodak, Rochester, NY, asks participants to choose one of the following groups by asking the following:

"Are you…

1. An Explorer? (learning the course material for the first time);

2. A Vacationer? (have seen the material before); or

3. A Prisoner? (forced to attend training)."

Boser says this question allows trainers to recognize expertise within the group (Vacationers) and gives those required to attend (Prisoners) a chance to release some of their frustrations before the session.

GAME #69: Bump

Game Categories:
☐ Opener ☐ Team-building
☑ Energizer ☑ Review
☐ Communication ☐ Topical

❖ **Purpose:** To energize participants and summarize key points at the end of a training session.

❖ **Time Required:** 5 minutes.

❖ **Size of Group:** Unlimited, but participants should work in small groups of four or five.

❖ **Materials Required:** Flipchart paper for each group; enough markers for everyone.

❖ **The Exercise in Action:** Mariana Luce, a trainer with Arbitron Co., in Beltsville, MD, uses a fast-moving game she calls "Bump." Here's how it works:

- Break people into teams of four or five.

- Give each team a one-minute timer (or a facilitator can keep time with a watch), flipchart paper, and five markers.

- The object is to list single words that summarize key training points (**Example:** A point about giving good feedback might be "timely").

- To win, a team needs to list the most words in one minute.

- Everyone gets a marker so that they can write words on their team's sheet as quickly as possible.

- After one minute, all writing stops.

- Teams then "bump" or cross out from their lists any words that appear on any other team's sheet.

- The team with the longest list of unduplicated key words wins.

Says Luce: "Everyone usually leaves the session laughing and energized, even if winning is the only prize."

GAME #70: License Plates

Game Categories:
- ☑ Opener
- ☐ Energizer
- ☐ Communication
- ☐ Team-building
- ☐ Review
- ☐ Topical

❖ **Purpose:** To creatively and visually get participants to introduce themselves.

❖ **Time Required:** 15 minutes.

❖ **Size of Group:** Unlimited.

❖ **Materials Required:** A blank "license plate," prepared in advance by the trainer; markers for the entire group.

❖ **The Exercise in Action:** At the beginning of her session, Jeanine Dederich, training manager of Associated Bank in Menomonee Falls, WI, gives each participant a form designed with the likeness of a blank license plate and asks them to create their own personalized plates, using no more than seven letters or numbers.

She then asks participants to introduce themselves to the rest of the group using their new "vanity" plate as a starting point. She asks each participant to give the group a few moments to "decode" the plate before explaining it, as some can be fairly tricky.

Some sample ideas are:

SLSMN = salesman
WKGMOM = working mom
DADOV3 = dad of three
INVSTR = investor
H20SKER = water skier

GAME #71: Get Through the Window

Game Categories:
- ☐ Opener
- ☐ Energizer
- ☐ Communication
- ☑ Team-building
- ☐ Review
- ☐ Topical

◆ **Purpose:** To involve participants in a physical demonstration of teamwork.

◆ **Time Required:** 20 minutes.

◆ **Size of Group:** Unlimited, but participants should work in small groups of four to seven.

◆ **Materials Required:** Flipchart paper; scissors; masking tape.

◆ **The Exercise in Action:** The "Get Through the Window" exercise can enhance team-building, says Dee Endelman, manager of human resources at Puget Sound Air Pollution Control in Seattle.

1. Tell your teams to take a break together.

2. Cut two pieces of flipchart paper into the shape of "Cs" and tape them together to create a "window" (shown below).

3. Tape the window across the doorframe of the room, high enough so that participants will need help getting through, and post a sign stating, "Get your team through the window without breaking it."

4. Call the team back. Observe discretely as they work to solve the problem.

5. When the team is "through the window," conduct a discussion on who did what in the process and how the others reacted to one another's roles.

Team-building 101:
Get your team through the window without breaking it.

Endelman says she often uses the exercise at department/management retreats because it provides people within work groups an avenue of communication in a non-threatening environment.

GAME #72: Rhythmic Sticks

Game Categories:
☐ Opener   ☑ Team-building
☑ Energizer   ☐ Review
☐ Communication   ☐ Topical

❖ **Purpose:** To help develop teamwork and cooperation.

❖ **Time Required:** 15 minutes.

❖ **Size of Group:** 12 to 15.

❖ **Materials Required:** 24 to 30 small sticks, about 18 inches in length; recording of rhythmic, relaxing music (CD or tape); music player.

❖ **The Exercise in Action:** Wendy Priestly, administrative training officer for NSW Fire Brigades, Sydney, Australia, provides each participant with a stick about 18 inches long and leads them through this team-building exercise:

Have participants pair up and ask each team to hold two sticks between them with their index fingers (as if they were pointing at each other, with the stick between the tips of their fingers). Play rhythmic relaxation music while partners close their eyes and move to the music, all the while holding the two sticks between their index fingers.

Next, have all the participants form a large circle with a stick between each person in the circle. Have them close their eyes and move to the music, while supporting the sticks with their index fingers.

Discuss the exercise. Ask participants how they felt as a team, how long it took to feel comfortable, how it felt to move into a larger group, and how it felt when they all were moving as one unit. Then tie the exercise back into the objective of the class by asking participants what conclusions/comparisons they can draw about the operation, formation, and development of a team.

GAME #73: Dealing with Harassment

Game Categories:
- ☐ Opener
- ☐ Energizer
- ☐ Communication
- ☐ Team-building
- ☐ Review
- ☑ Topical: Harassment

❖ **Purpose:** To help ease the tension during training about sexual harassment policies and make the material more interesting than a lengthy legal discourse.

❖ **Time Required:** 30 minutes.

❖ **Size of Group:** 5 to 10.

❖ **Materials Required:** The board game, *Harassment.*

❖ **The Exercise in Action:** Sexual harassment training can be intimidating for trainers as well as participants, and Theresa Baybutt, director of training for Designs, Inc., Chestnut Hill, MA, says a board game she uses helps.

The game is called *Harassment* and is sold in select retail stores (see information below). Here's how it works, in brief:

A "narrator"—usually the trainer—reads a potential harassment situation written on a game card to small groups of participants, who discuss among themselves whether they feel the situation is sexual harassment. Cards are provided to vote with. After further discussion among the whole class, the narrator provides the answer.

Baybutt has customized these generic game situations to match real situations that have occurred in her company, without providing names or places. She bought *Harassment* for all her field training personnel. "We've found it's a more effective and fun way to teach the material than having an expert lecture about it," she says.

Harassment is manufactured by T.D.C. Games of Itasca, IL, and sold for $20. For information on where to find the game or to order direct, call (800) 292-7676. Or write to T.D.C. Games, 1470 Norwood Drive, Itasca, IL 60143.

GAME #74: Hat Trick

Game Categories:	☐ Opener	☐ Team-building
	☐ Energizer	☐ Review
	☐ Communication	☑ Topical: Sales

❖ **Purpose:** To get sales trainees over their fear of role-playing exercises.

❖ **Time Required:** 30 minutes.

❖ **Size of Group:** 5 to 10.

❖ **Materials Required:** A hat or container to serve as an "idea collector."

❖ **The Exercise in Action:** Most people are uncomfortable role playing, even with topics they are familiar with. Sales trainees often battle the fear of not being knowledgeable enough, missing important points, not living up to their peers' expectations of their presentation skills, etc.

Edward Levitt, senior merchandising account representative for the 3M Corp., Signal Mountain, TN, tries to take some of the fear and tension out of role playing in his sales skills classes by using the "hat trick" method of matching topics to participants.

First, he has each participant write a "crazy" selling situation that could be performed in 5 to 10 minutes, such as "Sell an air conditioner at the North Pole," "Sell Mickey Mouse a better mousetrap," or "Sell Lee Iacocca a BMW." He puts all the ideas in a hat or other container and has each participant select one. He gives participants about 10 minutes to think about their topics and then randomly selects speakers to present their pitches.

"If you give participants a real product and ask them to give a sales presentation in front of their peers, they get very uneasy because they are all on different ability levels," Levitt says. "Putting them into out-of-the-ordinary situations with a very lighthearted atmosphere still shows their level of professionalism and how well they can think on their feet." Levitt says he primarily looks to see how creative participants can be in an unfamiliar situation and how they carry themselves during the presentation. "It's not how they say it, it is how they carry themselves as they give their presentation."

This technique can be used for other types of classes as well, by having participants submit topics/situations that stress creativity and spontaneity over knowledge about a particular topic or product.

GAME #75: Discovering Learning Styles

Game Categories:
☐ Opener   ☐ Team-building
☐ Energizer   ☐ Review
☐ Communication   ☑ Topical: Train-the-Trainer

❖ **Purpose:** To raise the consciousness of new trainers about the different ways trainees learn.

❖ **Time Required:** 20 to 30 minutes.

❖ **Size of Group:** 10 to 15.

❖ **Materials Required:** Flipchart paper and Lego building blocks.

❖ **The Exercise in Action:** Participants often bring widely varied learning styles to the classroom, and it's easy for new trainers to simply plow through a session without acknowledging those differences. So Mary Jessen, a training coordinator with Nintendo of America, Inc., Redmond, WA, uses these two exercises in her train-the-trainer session:

▼ Her training audience is typically supervisors scheduled to conduct cross-training for employees. To introduce them to the topic of learning styles and help them discover what their own style is, she gives a short quiz. Participants are asked to determine whether their style is visual, auditory, interactive, print, or hands-on.

She then posts graphics on flipcharts representing each of the five styles. For visual learners, she uses a large picture of a television; for auditory learners, a large ear; for interactive learners, the graphic is a group of people talking; for print learners, an open book; and for hands-on learners, she uses a picture of two hands. Participants are then given small colored dots and asked to place the dots on the flipchart of their own learning styles.

▼ To add more emphasis to the session, she uses another exercise featuring small Lego kits. It requires assembling about a dozen Lego parts into a small space vehicle. The kits are set up at five "stations" around the room. Participants then choose to assemble a kit based on instructions tailored to their learning style, or to a foreign style. For example, visual learners assemble their Lego kits using instructions that only have pictures, auditory learners assemble their kit by listening to instructions recorded on cassette players, and so on.

After the exercise, Jessen holds a discussion with the class about how easy or difficult it was to assemble the kits based on learning styles used.

GAME #76: Representative Objects

Game Categories:
☑ Opener ☐ Team-building
☐ Energizer ☐ Review
☐ Communication ☐ Topical

◆ **Purpose:** To get participants to think creatively at the outset of class.

◆ **Time Required:** 15 minutes.

◆ **Size of Group:** Unlimited.

◆ **Materials Required:** Paper and pencil for each participant.

◆ **The Exercise in Action:** As participants enter Melanie Casipe's classes, they are given a sheet of paper and a pencil. When everyone is seated, Casipe, a computer-based training specialist at Hudson's Bay Retail Group, Toronto, Ontario, asks them to consider what object best represents them and to draw it.

After all participants have finished their drawings, Casipe asks them to show their drawings to the class and complete this phrase: "If I were an object, I would be a... I chose this object because of its strengths in the areas of... However, it also has some weaknesses, such as... And just like me, this object tends to be..."

As a variation, Casipe asks participants to think of an animal instead of an object.

GAME #77: Rock Collection

Game Categories:	☑ Opener	☐ Team-building
	☐ Energizer	☐ Review
	☐ Communication	☑ Topical: Leadership

❖ **Purpose:** To show management trainees the importance of recognizing their own support style, their supervisor's management style, and how the two work together.

❖ **Time Required:** 15 minutes.

❖ **Size of Group:** 10 to 15.

❖ **Materials Required:** A large collection of rocks.

❖ **The Exercise in Action:** What good is a pile of rocks in a training classroom? Plenty, according to Linda Blevins, a training specialist at DuPont Corp. in LaPorte, TX. She uses rocks in her "Understanding Styles of Supervision" classes. The class is for people reporting to supervisors and for supervisors who report to supervisors.

At the beginning of the session, Blevins places a platter of rocks of all shapes, sizes, colors, and textures in the center of a table. She has participants choose a rock that most reminds them of their supervisor and then has participants explain why they chose that particular rock. Responses might include large and strong, overbearing and hard-headed, small and shiny, or rough on one side and smooth on the other.

After participants have described their supervisors' styles, Blevins discusses the three support and management styles:

Support Styles
- **Leader:** Independent, risk-taker, take charge person.
- **Facilitator:** Peace-maker, follows instructions to the letter.
- **Supporter:** Dependent, eager to please, passive.

Management Styles
- **Participative:** Allows others to make decisions, seeks input, wants results, but will adjust factors to get results.
- **Tell:** Makes all decisions, doesn't ask for input, results-oriented, risk-taker, doesn't like time wasted.
- **Delegative:** Decides only when forced, likes to empower and trust, gives freedom for people to act, wants results, but doesn't require details, expects others to take risks.

She then asks participants to ask themselves: Which style am I? What can I do about where I am today? What can I change? "People can predict and manage their reactions to supervisors, peers, and job pressures if they understand their own styles and their supervisors' styles," says

Blevins. For example, if your supervisor has a tell style and you have a leader support style, you're bound to clash.

Blevins says that once participants understand their perceptions of themselves and their supervisors, they can work together more cooperatively. "It comes down to the issue of control. Different management and support styles either crave it or disdain it."

Participants are invited to take their rocks back to the office with them and use them as paperweights. Blevins says the rocks are a great way to open the lines of communication. Blevins encourages participants to tell their supervisors—if they ask—the significance of the rock. "Honest communication builds respect and trust. And you have to have trust to build a good working relationship."

GAME #78: Pass the Hat

Game Categories:

☐ Opener   ☐ Team-building
☑ Energizer   ☑ Review
☐ Communication   ☐ Topical

❖ **Purpose:** To ensure that participants get a chance to share what they've learned.

❖ **Time Required:** 15 minutes.

❖ **Size of Group:** Unlimited.

❖ **Materials Required:** A hat or box to serve as an "idea collector."

❖ **The Exercise in Action:** After a topic is covered, or at the end of a session, Rick Bennett, a team leader trainer at CSARC, Windsor, CA, asks each participant to write down one valuable concept gleaned from the material and how it can be used. The ideas are tossed into a hat, box, or other convenient receptacle. After all have contributed, the hat is passed again, and each participant removes one note, putting it back and drawing again if it's the one he or she contributed. The ideas may be read aloud. The result: Everyone leaves with at least one useful concept and a way to use it.

GAME #79: Team Q & A

Game Categories:
- ☐ Opener
- ☐ Energizer
- ☐ Communication
- ☐ Team-building
- ☑ Review
- ☐ Topical

❖ **Purpose:** To help participants review and check their understanding of course topics.

❖ **Time Required:** 20 minutes.

❖ **Size of Group:** Unlimited, but participants should work in small groups of three to five.

❖ **Materials Required:** None.

❖ **The Exercise in Action:** Jim McCoy, area manager with Southwestern Bell Telephone, Irving, TX, asks each team to write five or six questions on the material just covered. Each team then asks questions of another team and rates the oppositions' answers on a scale of one (needs improvement) to five (excellent). A third team listens in and rates the quality of the questions in the same way.

Each team must ask and answer the same number of questions, one question at a time. Awarding prizes to the top team adds flavor to the game, McCoy says.

GAME #80: Memory Test

Game Categories:
- ☐ Opener
- ☐ Energizer
- ☐ Communication
- ☐ Team-building
- ☑ Review
- ☐ Topical

❖ **Purpose:** To use a combination of two well-known games—Tic-Tac-Toe and Bingo—to test participants' memories during review sessions.

❖ **Time Required:** 20 minutes.

❖ **Size of Group:** 10 to 15.

❖ **Materials Required:** List of course terms and definitions and a Tic-Tac-Toe grid, prepared in advance by the trainer.

❖ **The Exercise in Action:** Joyce Davis combines two familiar games—Tic-Tac-Toe and Bingo—to test the memories of her trainees.

Davis, a training coordinator at Nintendo of America in Redmond, WA, prepares a list of terms and their definitions, culled from the course material. At the end of the session, she gives each participant a list of terms numbered 1 through 10 and a sheet with a Tic-Tac-Toe grid printed on it. She then has participants write a number from 1 to 10 randomly in each square of the grid.

Next, Davis recites or uses an overhead to randomly show one definition at a time. Participants must match the definition to the numbered term on their lists so that the corresponding number can be crossed off the Tic-Tac-Toe grid. When three numbers in a straight or diagonal line are crossed off, the participant can call out "Bingo!" (see graphic).

In order to win a prize, the participant must also correctly recite the definition to each of the winning terms. An incorrect match of definition and term means the game continues.

A variation is to use 20 terms and two boards and have participants fill in all the squares on both grids.

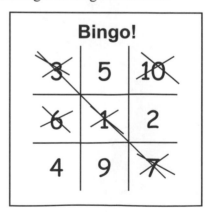

GAME #81: Wrenching Decisions

Game Categories:

- ☐ Opener
- ☐ Energizer
- ☑ Communication
- ☐ Team-building
- ☐ Review
- ☑ Topical: Supervisory

❖ **Purpose:** To show managers and supervisors the value of coaching skills.

❖ **Time Required:** 20 minutes.

❖ **Size of Group:** 12 to 15, but participants should work in small groups of 3 to 4.

❖ **Materials Required:** Small tool kits, including a six-piece wrench set; six nuts of varying sizes; prepared "performance situations."

❖ **The Exercise in Action:** Renee Collins, a trainer with Grainger Co. in Cincinnati, uses all the tools at her disposal—literally—when teaching coaching skills to managers and supervisors.

Each group of three to four participants receives a tool box, including a six-piece wrench set and six nuts of varying sizes. Each nut has a case study, or performance situation, attached to it that requires a particular response on the part of managers. Collins calls these, appropriately enough, "nutcases." Each wrench has an accompanying coaching skill taped to it, for example, skills such as praising, redirecting, constructively criticizing, negotiating, or resolving conflict.

Participants then choose a nut with its accompanying case study, read it, and determine which wrench, or coaching skill, to apply to address it best. For example, participants might get a situation where an employee is promoted into a new job and needs reassuring because of initial uncertainty. In this case, "praising" is the right coaching choice. Participants confirm if their choice is correct by seeing if the wrench size they choose fits the nut.

GAME #82: Ugly Chart Contest

Game Categories:
- ☐ Opener
- ☐ Energizer
- ☐ Communication
- ☐ Team-building
- ☐ Review
- ☑ Topical: Computer

❖ **Purpose:** To make the process of creating "artwork" less intimidating for participants.

❖ **Time Required:** 30 minutes.

❖ **Size of Group:** Unlimited.

❖ **Materials Required:** None, provided each participant has the proper hardware and software.

❖ **The Exercise in Action:** Creating a "beautiful" work of art can be intimidating for participants who are not artists. However, creating something ugly can be a fun challenge for participants.

William Wuttke, a trainer with the Federal Aviation Administration, uses "Ugly Chart Contest" to encourage exploration and creativity of participants in computer software classes. Wuttke provides the basics on charting a series of data for Microsoft Chart or Excel computer software. He then allows the class 30 minutes to explore the charting features to produce the "ugliest chart" possible.

Wuttke says participants get so engrossed with the contest that they don't want to stop. He has the participants choose the "ugliest chart" and awards a prize to the creator.

GAME #83: "Wanted" Posters

Game Categories:
- ☑ Opener
- ☐ Energizer
- ☐ Communication
- ☐ Team-building
- ☐ Review
- ☐ Topical

❖ **Purpose:** To introduce participants to one another in an unusual fashion.

❖ **Time Required:** 30 minutes.

❖ **Size of Group:** 10 to 15.

❖ **Materials Required:** "Wanted" posters (prepared in advance by the trainer) and a Polaroid camera.

❖ **The Exercise in Action:**
Participants in Craig Hauser's and Dale Morehouse's training courses at Walt Disney World, Orlando, FL, get to know one another via "Wanted" posters. Here's how it works:

Upon arrival, participants are given a "Wanted" poster like the one at right and asked to fill it out. The trainer collects the posters and tapes them to a wall. At the bottom of each sheet are a number of blanks. Participants are asked to circulate the room, read the posters, and mark at the bottom of each one who they think it describes.

The trainer, meanwhile, asks each participant to pose for two Polaroid photos, preferably out of sight of the rest of the class. The

```
┌─────────────────────────────┐
│          WANTED             │
│  ┌────────┐   ┌────────┐    │
│  │ Front  │   │  Side  │    │
│  │  mug   │   │  mug   │    │
│  │  shot  │   │  shot  │    │
│  └────────┘   └────────┘    │
│                             │
│ Background (information about family, │
│ place of birth, career information): │
│ ─────────────────────────── │
│ ─────────────────────────── │
│                             │
│ Known behaviors (hobbies): _____ │
│ ─────────────────────────── │
│                             │
│ Other points of interest (for example, │
│ "car last seen in" or "known to watch │
│ the following TV programs"): _____ │
│ ─────────────────────────── │
│                             │
│ Who could this be?          │
│ _____   _____   _____    │
└─────────────────────────────┘
```

shots are taken against the backdrop of a height marker similar to those shown in actual mug shots. Instead of holding a serial number, participants create tagboard signs displaying their first names and any "known alias," for example, "Nancy a.k.a. The Accountant."

After everyone has had photos taken and had a chance to guess whom the posters belong to, the trainer asks the participants to tape their photos in the appropriate places on their posters.

GAME #84: Musical Review

Game Categories:	☐ Opener	☐ Team-building
	☐ Energizer	☑ Review
	☐ Communication	☐ Topical

❖ **Purpose:** To share the best ideas from a series of sessions or course units.

❖ **Time Required:** 20 minutes.

❖ **Size of Group:** Unlimited.

❖ **Materials Required:** Several sheets of paper and a pen for each participant; a CD or tape and music player.

❖ **The Exercise in Action:** Susanne Moore, sales training and management development specialist for Great Western Bank, Chatsworth, CA, asks each participant to think of the most powerful ideas drawn from the course, write them on separate sheets of paper, and tape them to the walls throughout the room.

Moore then turns on some music and has participants play a modified version of musical chairs, called "musical review." She lets the music play while participants walk around the room in a clockwise direction to build up some energy. When she turns off the music, she has participants read the nearest idea sheet to the others. Participants remove those ideas from the wall and repeat the exercise until all the ideas have been read—and all but one participant has lost their "sheet" and sat down.

"By sharing someone else's idea, multiple ideas are reinforced," Moore says. "And adding music and movement creates an energizing review."

GAME #85: Awards Ceremony

Game Categories:
- ☐ Opener
- ☐ Energizer
- ☐ Communication
- ☐ Team-building
- ☑ Review
- ☐ Topical

❖ **Purpose:** To review course material and close training programs on an entertaining note.

❖ **Time Required:** 15 to 20 minutes.

❖ **Size of Group:** Unlimited.

❖ **Materials Required:** "Award ballots," prepared in advance by the trainer.

❖ **The Exercise in Action:** Guy Smith, program development and quality assurance representative at Walt Disney World, Lake Buena Vista, FL, holds an award ceremony to celebrate and discuss the most memorable course ideas.

Smith gives each participant five ballots for nominating a winner in each of these categories: *Idea Most Likely to Be Used, Best Comment Made in Class, Best Volunteer,* and *Best Activity.* Smith then holds a brief discussion about the winners.

GAME #86: Descriptors

Game Categories:
- ☑ Opener
- ☐ Energizer
- ☐ Communication
- ☑ Team-building
- ☐ Review
- ☐ Topical

❖ **Purpose:** To show participants how much they have in common with one another.

❖ **Time Required:** 15 minutes.

❖ **Size of Group:** Unlimited.

❖ **Materials Required:** Small slips of paper with personality descriptors on them, prepared in advance by the trainer.

❖ **The Exercise in Action:** Joyce Sarahan, a training specialist with the University of Texas Medical Branch, Galveston, TX, addresses pre-session stress and breaks the ice at the outset of class by creating small strips of paper with adjectives written on them that describe personality traits.

The strips may include: blunt, sensitive, intuitive, open-minded, judgmental, happy-go-lucky, and so on. Sarahan usually comes up with 10 to 15 descriptors (depending on the size of the group) and repeats each word individually on several strips.

As participants enter the room, they are asked to choose four words that best describe themselves, tape the strips to their name tags, then spend the first 15 minutes of class meeting and talking with people who have selected similar words.

In a variation for groups that know each other well, Sarahan asks participants to secretly tape on one another's backs words that best describe their co-workers. After five minutes or so of that activity, she asks participants to remove the strips from their backs and respond to two questions: Do you agree with how others view you? Were you surprised by any of the descriptors you found on your back?

GAME #87: "You Catch More Flies with Honey..."

**Game
Categories:**
☐ Opener
☐ Energizer
☑ Communication

☐ Team-building
☐ Review
☑ Topical

❖ **Purpose:** To show that force is not the most effective tool for communicating or for changing behavior.

❖ **Time Required:** 10 minutes.

❖ **Size of Group:** Unlimited, but participants should work in pairs.

❖ **Materials Required:** None.

❖ **The Exercise in Action:** The old adage, "You catch more flies with honey than vinegar," rings true in Debi Seddall's classes.

Seddall, an independent contractor/facilitator with KASET International in Bloomfield, MI, has participants pair up and face each other. She asks one person in each pair to close his or her hand and hold it clenched in front of the other. She then tells the second person to get the hand of the first person open as quickly as possible.

After 10 seconds, she asks them to stop. Most participants spent the time trying, unsuccessfully, to pry open their partners' fists with force; the more force they used, the more resistant their partners became.

Seddall asks whether others found less forceful ways to open their partners' hands. Generally someone comes up with the quickest and most agreeable solution to the problem: asking the partner, "Would you please open your hand?"

She leads the group in a discussion about effective management techniques to facilitate change—creatively, not forcefully—and to have open minds to others' ideas.

GAME #88: Tied Up in Knots

Game Categories:
- ☐ Opener
- ☐ Energizer
- ☐ Communication
- ☑ Team-building
- ☐ Review
- ☐ Topical

❖ **Purpose:** To demonstrate the effect one person's actions have on others.

❖ **Time Required:** 10 to 15 minutes.

❖ **Size of Group:** Unlimited, but participants should work in small groups of 4 to 10.

❖ **Materials Required:** Several balls of twine.

❖ **The Exercise in Action:** To make her point about teamwork, Becky Schaefer, a manager of employee involvement at U.S. West, Denver, gives one person in each small group a ball of twine. That person holds onto the end and passes the ball to another team member, and so on, until everyone in the small group is holding the strand at some point—keeping it taut without breaking it. Participants are encouraged to loop the twine around a person or two in the group to further complicate the equation, returning the ball to the first person to complete the circuit after all are connected.

The teams are then asked to experiment with movement. What happens when one person moves her hand to the left two feet? What happens if someone sits down? What sort of cooperation is necessary for the group to move across the room—all the while adhering to the objective of keeping the string taut without breaking it.

After several minutes, Schaefer asks what was learned. Did the string ever break? If so, why? Were some people forceful while others were accommodating? Did leaders develop? Too many of them? What kinds of communication worked? What didn't?

The main point, she says, is to demonstrate that every action a team member makes, no matter how insignificant it might seem, has an effect on others.

GAME #89: Tricky Drawings

Game Categories:
- ☐ Opener
- ☐ Energizer
- ☐ Communication
- ☐ Team-building
- ☐ Review
- ☑ Topical: Train-the-Trainer

◆ **Purpose:** To demonstrate to participants that they don't need to be artists to have professional-looking visuals.

◆ **Time Required:** 15 minutes.

◆ **Size of Group:** Unlimited.

◆ **Materials Required:** "Trick" flipchart pages, prepared in advance by the trainer.

◆ **The Exercise in Action:** Maria Yester, manager of training and development at West Virginia University in Morganton, WV, plays a "trick" on participants in her train-the-trainer classes:

Yester prepares several flipchart pages for the "trick" before class by faintly tracing an intricate cartoon and putting a blank flipchart page in front of each. The tracing is visible to Yester and not the audience. When she talks about using flipcharts in class as an effective teaching tool, she claims that anyone can be a Picasso. She then quickly traces a cartoon and flips to a new sheet of paper (without a tracing underneath) and asks for a volunteer to try drawing the cartoon. Of course, the group "volunteers" someone.

The volunteer attempts to copy the cartoon she has drawn. Yester then announces to the group that the volunteer is going to attend a "mini art school." She pulls the volunteer out of class and explains how she did her drawing. With another tracing ready, she instructs the volunteer to go back into the room and press the sheet on top of the tracing until the faint pencil markings show through so that it can be quickly traced over with a marker. The other participants are shocked. Of course, they can see the vast improvement in the volunteer's "ability" and know there is a trick, but are unsure how it is done. Yester then explains and demonstrates the technique, emphasizing that even someone who can't draw can easily produce professional flipcharts.

GAME #90: Trading Cards

Game Categories:
☐ Opener   ☑ Team-building
☑ Energizer   ☐ Review
☐ Communication   ☐ Topical

❖ **Purpose:** To improve team-building skills.

❖ **Time Required:** 10 to 20 minutes.

❖ **Size of Group:** Unlimited.

❖ **Materials Required:** A large supply of 3 x 5 inch index cards.

❖ **The Exercise in Action:** Cindy Jones hands out three index cards to each participant. They are asked to write down three behaviors they would realistically like to change in their work-a-day lives—one behavior per card.

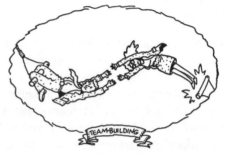

Jones then collects, shuffles, and deals out the cards again so that each participant ends up with three cards. Participants are asked to walk around the room and make "trades," picking cards that fit themselves or that are good ideas. (**Note:** Make sure participants are given ample time to make these trades.)

Participants are then asked to choose one card as a "keeper," committing to put that card in a location they will see on the job or at home every day for at least a month, Jones says, "and at the same time committing to changing that particular behavior."

GAME #91: Scavenger Hunt

Game Categories:
- ☐ Opener
- ☐ Energizer
- ☐ Communication
- ☐ Team-building
- ☐ Review
- ☑ Topical: Orientation

❖ **Purpose:** To introduce new employees to other divisions during orientation training.

❖ **Time Required:** 20 to 30 minutes.

❖ **Size of Group:** Unlimited, but participants should work in teams of three to six.

❖ **Materials Required:** "Scavenger lists," prepared in advance by the trainer.

❖ **The Exercise in Action:** As part of her organization's orientation training, Margaret Wheeler, a trainer with the product and sales division of The Body Shop in Chicago, sends teams of new employees throughout the company on a scavenger hunt.

Teams are given a list of objects that can be found in various departments, which Wheeler has preplanted with the help of key people in those departments. When teams report back to class, the objects are used to discuss the different divisions of the company and how they interrelate. Teams are then asked to create a "work of art" from the objects that embodies the company's spirit as they perceive it.

Game Categories:
☐ Opener
☐ Energizer
☑ Communication
☑ Team-building
☐ Review
☐ Topical

❖ **Purpose:** To foster communication and networking among participants.

❖ **Time Required:** 15 minutes.

❖ **Size of Group:** Unlimited.

❖ **Materials Required:** Several different children's puzzles, with the pieces all mixed together.

❖ **The Exercise in Action:** David Plantier, owner of Boiler & Combustion Seminars, Bloomington, MN, uses this simple exercise as a motivator in his classroom:

Plantier mixes the pieces from children's puzzles—a different puzzle for each table in the room—in a bag. As participants enter, he has them select a puzzle piece at random.

After participants are seated, he asks them to show him all the puzzle pieces at each table. He gives each table a frame, and exchanges pieces as necessary so that no one has a piece that fits the frame at his or her own table.

Shortly before the first break, Plantier explains his intent:

"As your trainer, I do not have the answers to all your questions. If life is a puzzle, I do not have all the pieces. I have a few, but you have many more. To complete the puzzle on your table, you must circulate during breaks and lunch to find the answers (pieces).

"Learning is an exchange. To get a piece of your puzzle, you must exchange information with someone. Share a helpful hint, ask a question and find the answer, or simply tell someone how you will use an idea from the seminar. The first group to complete a puzzle wins."

If people look confused, Plantier demonstrates by asking for someone to give him one idea from the session they plan to use back on the job. The first participant to respond gets a puzzle piece (Plantier keeps some puzzle pieces so that participants have to come to him for ideas, too).

After the break, Plantier gives a sack of candy to the table with the most pieces in place.

GAME #93: Toys in the Attic

Game Categories:
- ☑ Opener
- ☑ Energizer
- ☐ Communication
- ☐ Team-building
- ☑ Review
- ☐ Topical

❖ **Purpose:** To challenge participants to think creatively and work smarter.

❖ **Time Required:** 10 minutes.

❖ **Size of Group:** Unlimited.

❖ **Materials Required:** A paddle with a ball attached to it by an elastic string.

❖ **The Exercise in Action:** Toys are a staple in most training rooms. Pam Wooldridge enlists the help of a toy easily found in most stores: a paddle with a ball attached to it by an elastic string.

At the end of a day or an individual learning unit, she asks for a volunteer to review a set of points made in class *while keeping the ball in motion* (those are her exact instructions). Most try to bounce the ball against the paddle, but soon realize that Wooldridge's only stipulation was to keep the ball moving. Soon, she says, participants are swinging the ball until it is wrapped around the paddle or making it sway back and forth like a pendulum.

After the review, Wooldridge, a training specialist for Strouds, City of Industry, CA, makes the point that the exercise shows that people often try to make a task more difficult than it needs to be, and that by thinking creatively, they can come up with better ways of doing things.

Note: The exercise can also be used as a session opener or energizer, with participants instructed to keep the ball in motion while they introduce themselves. Again, the exercise ultimately teaches them to work smarter.

GAME #94: Say What?

Game Categories:
- ☐ Opener
- ☐ Energizer
- ☑ Communication
- ☐ Team-building
- ☑ Review
- ☐ Topical

❖ **Purpose:** To teach a lesson about the importance of well-organized communication.

❖ **Time Required:** 10 minutes.

❖ **Size of Group:** Unlimited, but participants should work in small groups of four to six.

❖ **Materials Required:** Scissors for each group, and a copy of a "letter," prepared in advance by the trainer.

❖ **The Exercise in Action:** By jumbling the sentences of a "simple," six-sentence letter and asking participants to arrange the letter as they think it was meant to read, Jim Chandler makes a point about clear communication.

He divides the class into groups of four to six members and gives each a pair of scissors and a copy of the rearranged letter to each group (see examples on the opposite page). The letter can be on any topic related to the subject matter at hand, or something unrelated and humorous to add fun to the exercise.

Chandler gives the groups 10 minutes to complete the task, after which he asks each group to select a leader to read the group's page aloud. The letters can come out with surprisingly different meanings, simply by having one or two sentences switched around.

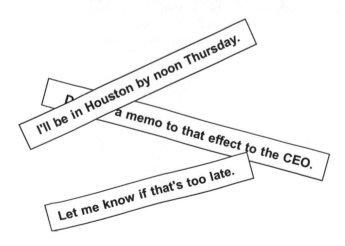

Chandler, a training consultant with Metropolitan Life Insurance, Southfield, MI, originally used this exercise in sessions dealing specifically with writing, but has found it useful in a number of areas where the importance of clear communication is part of the message. Because participants have so much fun with it, he says he sometimes uses it as an ice breaker in classes where it has no thematic tie-in at all.

Cutting and pasting the same sentences in a different order can convey a radically different message.

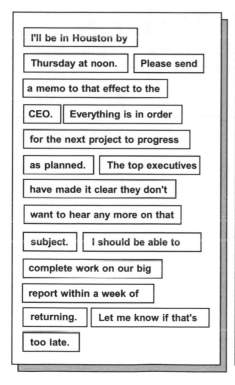
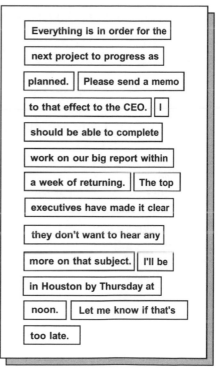

GAME #95: Mannerisms

Game Categories:	☐ Opener	☐ Team-building
	☐ Energizer	☐ Review
	☐ Communication	☑ Topical: Train-the-Trainer

❖ **Purpose:** To help new trainers avoid using mannerisms that can distract a class during a training presentation.

❖ **Time Required:** 10 minutes.

❖ **Size of Group:** Unlimited, but participants should work in small groups of five to seven.

❖ **Materials Required:** Flipcharts with easels for each group.

❖ **The Exercise in Action:** John Kane, manager of training and development for Traco Co., in Zelienople, PA, uses this flipchart activity in his train-the-trainer classes:

He first places a number of flipchart easels back to back, with the word "mannerisms" spelled out in all upper-case letters, vertically on each pad. Participants are divided into teams, and each team is positioned in front of a flipchart easel, blocking its view of what other teams are writing on their charts.

Teams are given 90 seconds to fill in words or phrases of common distracting mannerisms that begin with one letter of the word "mannerisms."

If a team assigns a mannerism to each letter in the allotted time, everyone receives a prize—a small squeeze change purse—as a reminder of one mannerism to be avoided—*jingling coins in the pockets.*

The lists are then posted in plain view, to be used later as a reference when participants provide feedback to each other during videotaped practice sessions.

GAME #96: Building Blocks

Game Categories:
- ☐ Opener
- ☐ Energizer
- ☑ Communication
- ☐ Team-building
- ☐ Review
- ☐ Topical

❖ **Purpose:** To help improve communication skills and raise consciousness about treating customers with empathy.

❖ **Time Required:** 15 minutes.

❖ **Size of Group:** Unlimited, but participants should work in small groups of five to seven.

❖ **Materials Required:** Multiple sets of Lego building blocks; photos of a Lego model; and several blindfolds.

❖ **The Exercise in Action:** Andy Oman, training and development administrator for Hoffman Engineering, Anoka, MN, uses an exercise featuring a blindfold and Lego toys.

He first has his entire class study a preconstructed Lego model, often in the form of a plane or house, for one minute. Then one participant in a group of five to seven is blindfolded while other members disassemble the model. Using a photo of the model as a reference, group members instruct the blindfolded participant in reconstructing the model. Team members cannot hand pieces to the blindfolded member. Typical commands include things such as "feel for the two-inch wide tile and place at the far left corner." Oman usually allows two to four minutes for assembly.

Oman makes the point that new levels of understanding and communication skills are necessary for dealing with internal and external customers.

GAME #97: Judge Mental

**Game
Categories:**
- ☐ Opener
- ☐ Energizer
- ☐ Communication
- ☐ Team-building
- ☐ Review
- ☑ Topical: Sales

❖ **Purpose:** To help educate sales representatives about asking effective questions in sales situations.

❖ **Time Required:** 20 to 30 minutes.

❖ **Size of Group:** 10 to 15.

❖ **Materials Required:** A judge's gavel.

❖ **The Exercise in Action:** Asking probing yet sensitive questions is a critical skill for salespeople, and nothing can upset a sales prospect more than having to field judgmental questions. Lynn Tiutczenko, a training and development specialist with Northwestern Mutual Life in Milwaukee, uses a trainer-led discussion accompanied by videotapes on developing questioning skills. Participants are then given a chance to practice what they've learned by participating in a "Judge Mental" exercise.

The trainer selects one participant—or possibly a participant's supervisor—to act as "Judge Mental," an authority figure who is given a sign displaying his or her title, a designated table or "bench" at the front of the room, and a gavel. The trainer acts as the sales prospect or client, and the participants act collectively as the agent. (This exercise can be adapted for service training by creating a role-play scenario and having participants act as customer service representatives.)

Participants use a company fact-finder as the basis for their questioning; their mission is to develop a sense of the client's needs. It is Judge Mental's task to listen to each question and, if it is worded or delivered in judgmental fashion, to rap on the table with the gavel to stop the questioning. The Judge then explains why the question needs to be improved, and participants put their heads together to formulate a more appropriate question.

Each person asks questions for a set number of minutes, and either trainer or participants serve as timekeeper. Typically, the exercise lasts 30 minutes, so if there are 15 participants, each asks questions for about two minutes.

Tiutczenko says participants enjoy hearing how peers formulate and ask questions, and for the trainer it's a fun way to test participants' understanding of questioning skills and concepts.

GAME #98: The Right Chemistry

Game Categories:
- ☐ Opener
- ☐ Energizer
- ☐ Communication
- ☑ Team-building
- ☐ Review
- ☐ Topical

❖ **Purpose:** To show there are two distinct viewpoints in any conflict.

❖ **Time Required:** 10 to 15 minutes.

❖ **Size of Group:** Unlimited.

❖ **Materials Required:** Three transparent glass beakers or test tubes filled with water; small packets of sugar and salt; colored glass marbles.

❖ **The Exercise in Action:** T. J. Titcomb, director of training at Family Service, Lancaster, PA, begins her team-building/conflict resolution classes with a discussion on the need to change expectations about conflict. Rather than assuming that conflict is only negative, she teaches participants to see it as a motivator for change and a tool to ensure that all viewpoints are considered.

Titcomb then sets up her supplies at the front of the class and demonstrates the difference between "soluble" (solvable) conflicts and "insoluble" (unsolvable) conflicts:

"Any conflict," she explains, "has two distinct viewpoints. Some conflicts are 'soluble.' The two parts combine, they don't disappear—they become something new, keeping the best of both." (She pours a small amount of sugar into a beaker of water and shakes it.)

"Some conflicts are sweet because they are easily resolved through collaboration." (She pours a small amount of salt into the second beaker of water and shakes it.)

"Other conflicts add spice to life. They are a little harder and take more effort to resolve. In time they might reappear again as the two parts separate. We might have to return later and work at them again to keep them soluble." (She shakes the beaker a second time.)

(She then holds up the third water beaker, drops in a glass marble, and shakes it.) "But we must also recognize that some conflicts cannot be resolved. What can we do when faced with insoluble conflicts? They can be understood, appreciated, and accepted. We step back and admire the diversity of ideas, opinions, and values among human beings. We learn that different is okay. We also decide as individuals when to stop trying to force solutions onto insoluble conflicts. We are then free to put our energy into changing our reaction to people."

GAME #99: Candy-Buying Experience

Game Categories:	☐ Opener	☐ Team-building
	☐ Energizer	☐ Review
	☐ Communication	☑ Topical: Customer Satisfaction

❖ **Purpose:** To emphasize that in customers' eyes, "product value" means more than just an equitable price.

❖ **Time Required:** 20 minutes.

❖ **Size of Group:** 10 to 15.

❖ **Materials Required:** Three different types of candy.

❖ **The Exercise in Action:** Depending on situation and need, customers have widely differing expectations of products and services that salespeople need to address. To make a point about that issue, Sandy Freeman, a retail trainer with First Federal Savings Bank in LaCrosse, WI, uses this exercise:

After a short introduction, she asks her participants to take part in a "taste test." Freeman then hands out a "Sampler's Taste Test Sheet" and three different samples of candy—chocolate truffles, chocolate mints, and bite-size Tootsie Rolls—asking each participant to comment on the quality and taste of each. She then asks all to choose their favorites; most participants pick the truffles.

Freeman then provides them with the following information on cost and packaging of the candy:

- Sample A, the truffles, cost $7 for seven pieces and come in a dull gray box.
- Sample B, the mints, cost $6 per pound and come in a foil-wrapped gift box with a card.
- Sample C, the Tootsie Rolls, cost $2.29 for 16 ounces and come in a plastic bag.

Given that information, participants are then asked which candy they would purchase in the following situations (these can be changed to fit the diversity of the group):

1. Which would you purchase as a gift for your mother-in-law?
2. Which would you purchase to send with your six-year-old to school as a treat?
3. Which would you purchase for your spouse to celebrate a big promotion?

Freeman says it typically surprises everyone how small a role price plays in their decision to buy one candy over another.

GAME #100: Ad Campaign

Game Categories:
- ☐ Opener
- ☑ Energizer
- ☐ Communication
- ☐ Team-building
- ☑ Review
- ☐ Topical

❖ **Purpose:** To tap participants' creative juices by encouraging them to use newly learned material.

❖ **Time Required:** 20 minutes.

❖ **Size of Group:** Unlimited, but participants should work in small groups of five to seven.

❖ **Materials Required:** Flipchart paper and markers for each group.

❖ **The Exercise in Action:** Jack Redfield splits his class into small groups and gives each group several sheets of flipchart paper and markers. He asks each group to pick a benefit they have learned from any other class module and create a magazine or newspaper advertisement promoting its benefits with text and drawings.

Redfield, a customer contact specialist with Rochester Gas & Electric, Rochester, NY, says the activity is a very effective review tool and that he is amazed at the variety of ideas displayed in the "ads."

GAME #101: Your 2¢ Worth

Game Categories:	☐ Opener	☐ Team-building
	☑ Energizer	☐ Review
	☐ Communication	☐ Topical

❖ **Purpose:** To combat negativity in the classroom as it occurs and show how to handle it in the workplace.

❖ **Time Required:** An ongoing exercise.

❖ **Size of Group:** Unlimited.

❖ **Materials Required:** A roll (or two) of pennies.

❖ **The Exercise in Action:** When participants get caught up in airing complaints—about supervisors, workloads, whatever—to the point that the course is hindered by it, Sandy Stevenson, training and employee services manager at Slippery Rock University, Slippery Rock, PA, muffles the negativity with a roll of pennies.

She gives each participant two coins. Questions and comments pertaining directly to the class are free, she tells them. But anyone wanting to gripe or complain has to spend one of their pennies to do so. Once they have "put in their two cents' worth," no more complaints are allowed from them.

The result, she says, is that most people don't grouse at all, because they're afraid of running out of pennies and being unable to talk when they have what they consider to be a really important complaint.

This method keeps control in the hands of the instructor, she says, without stifling feedback and dissent entirely.

R obert Pike has been developing and implementing training programs
for business, industry, government, and other professions since 1969.
As president of Creative Training Techniques International, Inc.,
Resources for Organizations, Inc., and The Resources Group, Inc., he leads
more than 150 sessions each year on topics such as leadership, attitudes,
motivation, communication, decision-making, problem-solving, personal
and organizational effectiveness, conflict management, team-building, and
managerial productivity.

More than 50,000 trainers have attended Pike's Creative Training
Techniques workshops. As a consultant, he has worked with such
organizations as American Express, Upjohn, Hallmark Cards, Inc., IBM,
PSE&G, Bally's Casino Resort, and Shell Oil. A member of the American
Society for Training and Development (ASTD) since 1972, he has served
on three of the organization's national design groups, and held office as
director of special interest groups and as a member of the national board.

An outstanding speaker, Pike has been a presenter at regional and
national conferences for ASTD and other organizations. He currently
serves as co-chairman of the Professional Emphasis Groups for the
National Speakers' Association. He has been granted the professional
designation of Certified Speaking Professional (CSP) by the NSA, an
endorsement earned by only 170 of the organization's 3,800 members.

Pike is editor of Lakewood Publications' *Creative Training
Techniques Newsletter*, is author of *The Creative Training Techniques
Handbook*, and has contributed articles to *TRAINING Magazine, The
Personnel Administrator*, and *Self-Development Journal*. He has been
listed, since 1980, in *Who's Who in the Midwest* and is listed in *Who's
Who in Finance and Industry*.